D0875576

TOMORROW IS HERE

TOMORROW IS HERE

THE MISSION AND WORK OF THE CHURCH
AS SEEN FROM THE MEETING OF
THE INTERNATIONAL MISSIONARY COUNCIL
AT WHITBY, ONTARIO, JULY 5-24, 1947

KENNETH SCOTT LATOURETTE
and
WILLIAM RICHEY HOGG

PUBLISHED FOR THE
International Missionary Council
by FRIENDSHIP PRESS: NEW YORK

KENNETH SCOTT LATOURETTE, Ph.D., D.D., Litt.D., LL.D., a native of Oregon, received his academic training at Linfield College and at Yale University. After serving as a traveling secretary for the Student Volunteer Movement, he taught for two years at Yale-in-China, Changsha. He was a lecturer and assistant professor of history at Reed College and for four years an associate and then a full professor of history at Denison University. Since 1921, Dr. Latourette has been teaching at Yale University, where he is the D. Willis James Professor of Missions and Oriental History. During the autumn of 1947 he gave the Cadbury Lectures at the University of Birmingham, England. He is president of the American Historical Association.

Dr. Latourette has made extensive studies in and has had first-hand contacts with the international mission movement and is the author of many well known books on missions and other subjects, among them being his monumental seven-volume *History of the Expansion of Christianity, Missions Tomorrow, The Chinese: Their History and Culture, The History of Japan* (1947), and *A Short History of the Far East*. He attended the Madras meeting of the International Missionary Council in 1938 as well as the meeting of that organization held at Whitby, Ontario, in the summer of 1947.

WILLIAM RICHEY HOGG, B.A., B.D., a Pennsylvanian, was educated at Duke University and Yale University. He is at present the Dwight Fellow of Yale Divinity School, majoring under Dr. Latourette in the Graduate School of Yale University. His doctoral dissertation, *A History of the International Missionary Council*, is expected to be completed before he leaves for China in 1949 as a missionary under the auspices of the Board of Missions of the Methodist Church. He is a member of the National Committee of the Interseminary Movement and has spent a year as its traveling secretary, visiting one hundred and seventeen seminaries in the United States and Canada.

To

JOHN R. MOTT

Quorum pars magna fuit

CONTENTS

PREFACE

TOMORROW IS HERE. We are in the midst of a new age. For years we have been saying that we are living in the twilight of a dying world and that the new world is about to be born. We have been hearing descriptions of what that new world is to be. We have attempted to say what the Christian program in this world of the future should be. Indeed, eleven years ago one of the authors of this book wrote a little volume that he called *Missions Tomorrow*. That tomorrow has come. The new age has dawned. We may not like this new age. It has in it much of uncertainty and even of terror. These are among its outstanding features. Yet all of us who are now living must face this tomorrow. We cannot escape it.

We who are Christians have the privilege — and the obligation — of entering the new world as the bearers of the Gospel. By the very fact that we have accepted the Gospel — if we have *really* accepted it and are not passively assenting to it as an inheritance from Christian parents and a Christian environment — we are saying that it is true and that in it are the secret of life and the hope of mankind.

As Christians, in a very special sense we affirm that tomorrow is here. We pray, as our Lord taught us: "Thy kingdom come, thy will be done, on earth as it is in heaven." We look for the coming of God's kingdom. By that we mean, as the most familiar petition of our faith has implied, a human society, a social order, in which God is unquestionably king, in which his will is fully done, in which men are perfect as their Father in heaven is perfect. Even the most casual glance at our world reveals the tragic fact that God's will is not fully done. The mass of mankind is still in rebellion against its rightful ruler. Yet even in the days of his flesh our Lord declared that the kingdom of God was in the midst of men and that it was possible even then for men to enter it, as by a new birth. God's kingdom is a present reality. Yet it is clear that it is not fully come and that it is also a future hope. In this sense Christians affirm that God's kingdom, for the full realization of which all creation groans and is in travail, has already begun. It is by no means consummated or completed. Yet it is already in the making. Even now the tomorrow for which the Christian longs is in part here.

Both the new age and the presence in it of God's kingdom were vividly seen in an event in the summer of 1947. Like so much of the operation of God's spirit, this event was unspectacular, and was vivid only to those who were prepared to appreciate its significance. In the quiet village of Whitby, Ontario, in the modest building of the Ontario Ladies' College, during part of the month of July, a small company — only slightly over a hundred in number — gathered under the auspices of the International Missionary Council. Yet this company was from forty nations and from many different races. It included Germans who only a few months before were regarded as enemies by the governments of most of the delegates. About a third were from what are often termed the "younger churches" — those churches that have arisen from the missions of the past century and a half. This in itself was a foreshadowing of the world church, evidence that tomorrow is here. Today the overwhelming majority of Christians are in the so-called "older churches," those of Europe, America, and Australasia. That a third of the Whitby gathering were from the "younger churches" was a prophecy of the church that is to be, in which European and American memberships will no longer predominate.

The remarkable unity of the gathering was also striking evidence that tomorrow is here. The delegates were from many denominations — Anglican, Baptist, Lutheran, Congregationalist, Presbyterian, Methodist, and other denominations that represent the opposites within Protestantism. Here were representatives of what are generally regarded as exploited and exploiting nations — Indians and British, Filipinos and Americans, a Fijian and white Australians, Negroes from Africa, and Belgians and English. Yet all worked and worshiped together and discussed controversial issues with a harmony that seasoned conference-goers declared they had never seen equaled. Here was that world church that faith tells us is to be — from every kindred and tribe, with wide variety in forms of worship and organization — knit together in love by simple faith in Christ and unwavering loyalty to him.

Here, too, was quiet confidence born of the sense of the presence of God's spirit. There was no blinking of the grim facts of our tragic age. These were faced in all their starkness. Coming from almost all parts of the world as the delegates did, many from lands devastated by war and some with recent experience of concentration camps and prisons, they knew all too well those phases of our age that for many of their contemporaries spell frustration and despair. Yet at Whitby, in contrast, was a sense of high adventure and of undaunted hope. The tomorrow that is here is even now the scene of God's ceaseless redemptive love. The conference was marked by resolute plans for giving the Gospel to the entire world. The "evangelization of the world in this generation," not many years before regarded as an obsolete shibboleth, was declared by the delegates to be both a possibility and an obligation.

It is the world, the Gospel, and the church as seen from Whitby that constitute the theme of this little book. We who write it had the high privilege of being at Whitby from the initial session through the last of the committees that planned the next steps ahead. Yet in it is no day-by-day report of a conference. Such a transcription could never catch the full spirit or significance of what was there. The book is, rather, an attempt to portray the tomorrow that is here as it was seen from that gathering. First we will endeavor to set forth the world and the present state of the church the globe around as they were described at Whitby. This will be followed by a description of the company that gathered there and of the historical development out of which it arose as the miniature of the world church that is both already in being and is to be. Then will come an account of the eternal Gospel of which the church is the messenger. Finally there will be outlined the plans that were laid at Whitby for carrying out the church's commission in the tomorrow that is already here.

By a strange coincidence, the name Whitby has an earlier occurrence in the history of the church. In 664, there convened in Whitby, England, a gathering at which a decision was reached that helped to bring the church in England into closely knit fellowship with the church on the adjacent continent, and thus into the company that embraced the Christians of the Western world. In Whitby, Canada, in 1947, another milepost was passed in the progress of a fellowship that is not confined to Europe but is even now as wide as the inhabited world. In that comparison and that contrast is vividly seen the hope of the tomorrow that is here.

Chapter One

THE WORLD OF TOMORROW
IS HERE

THE WORLD THAT IS HERE IS ONE OF STRIKING CONTRASTS. It is one of fear and yet of hope. But this paradox has been true in every age. Man's road has always been rough. From the dawn of his existence he has been confronted with peril, but peril that some of his number, through resourcefulness and resolution, have turned into gain. Although he has survived, as a well known recent play has reminded us, "by the skin of his teeth," he has grown in numbers and in material wealth. In the tomorrow that is here, danger and hope are accentuated and combined to a peculiar degree. As never before in recorded history, mankind is bound together in the bundle of life. Ours is a shrunken world. Because of the prodigious strides in transportation and communication during the past century and a half, and especially during our generation, the human race has been knit into a perilous and contradictory unity. The unity is one of discord, enhanced by the very fact of forced intimate association. The disorders of one segment affect the whole. If one member suffers, all the members suffer with it. It is literally and tragically true that mankind may destroy itself. Nevertheless, the possibilities for collective advance for the entire race were never so great.

This mixture of threat and opportunity displays a variety of aspects, but it must be faced at the very outset of any attempt to understand the tomorrow that is here. Those who gathered at Whitby were well aware of it. Their discussions had it consciously in the background.

Revolution Is Here

First of all, the age is one of revolution. The old and familiar are passing. The new is being born. Revolution is not a novel human experience. It has been seen again and again in many segments of mankind. What is without precedent is the degree to which it is affecting every phase of man's life. Moreover, the pace is quickening. Through most of the present century revolution has been spectacular. It has been speeding up in recent years. The revolution has its center in the Occident. Here the old culture is dying and the new is not yet in being. The familiar Western civilization is passing. Since in the past four centuries it has spread throughout the earth, its disorders are affecting all the race. A world civilization seems in the process of birth, but the travail is sharp and the issue is not yet clear.

The revolution is in part political. It includes the disappearance of ruling houses, once seemingly enduring features of the political firmament but now almost forgotten — those of the sultans of Turkey, of the Hohenzollerns, of the Hapsburgs, of the Romanovs, of the Manchu imperial line, and of the House of Savoy; and the substitution of quite different regimes — those of the Young Turks, of the Second and the Third Reich followed by Allied occupation and partition, of the various states that once composed the Austrian Empire, of the Union of Soviet Socialist Republics under the dictation of the Communist party, of the Republic of China, and of the republic in

Italy. It embraces the collapse of the Japanese Empire and the attempted remaking of the government of the home islands under the supervision of the victors.

The revolution is even more pronounced in realms other than political. It is evident in the progress of industrialization, in the complete shift of the basis of education in China, in the threatened disintegration of the family, in the breakup of the tribal structure in Africa, in the decay of historic religions, as in Turkey, China, Japan, and parts of Europe, and in the accompanying interrogation of long-accepted bases of morals. These are but samples. The list could be greatly prolonged.

Revolution means the decline or disappearance of the old. Now, as in other ages, it means suffering for many and sometimes even moral shipwreck for others. Yet it also gives opportunity for shaping a new and better order.

The Decline of Western Europe and the Freeing of Subject Peoples

Closely related phases of the revolution are the decline of western Europe and the freeing of peoples who were once subject to the Occident.

Between four and five centuries ago western Europeans began the expansion by which they have dominated the globe. Their control was accelerated in the nineteenth century. Western European peoples settled the Americas, Australia, and New Zealand. They subdued most of Asia, Africa, and the islands of the Pacific. The impact of the culture of western Europe was the chief cause of the revolution among non-European cultures.

As we have suggested, western Europe is desperately ill. Western civilization is passing. The two world wars of the present century were symptoms of a deep-seated sickness, and they aggravated that sickness. In the tomorrow that is here western Europe will not have the proud superiority that so recently seemed one of the axioms of the world scene.

For Christians the decline of western Europe is peculiarly sobering. Western Europe has been the center of what we have been accustomed to call Christendom. It is the region in which Christianity has long been the prevailing religion, and from which for the past five centuries it has had its chief spread. Does this decline mean that Christianity, the historic center of its power weakened, is to wane as a force in mankind? What does it indicate of the ability of Christianity to save civilization? These are two questions that will not down. We must recur to them later.

With the decay of western Europe, the hold which that portion of the world has had on non-European peoples is being relaxed. European imperialism is waning. People after people, long restive, are achieving their political independence. India, Burma, and possibly Ceylon seem to be on their way out of the British Empire. Eire has gained autonomy from Britain, and Egypt is seeking it. Syria and Lebanon are independent of France; Indo-China is demanding independence. Indonesia is moving out from under Dutch control. Even the United States, strong though it is, has heeded the trend, and has granted independence to the Philippines, and is troubled by the agitation in Puerto Rico, which demands either admission to the Union as a state or full independence. China has freed herself from extraterritoriality and almost all other phases of the "unequal treaties." In some European possessions south of the Sahara, Africans are being granted a larger measure of self-government. They are widely restive under the white man's yoke. Only in Japan, Korea, and to a less degree in Manchuria has the control of the Occident been recently augmented, and that change in control has been either by the United States or Russia, neither of which is a Western European power.

The freeing of non-Europeans can mean added disorder. On the other hand, it can make for enhanced self-respect and responsibility. As we are to see, these goals are already being accompanied by the emergence of a world Christian community in which non-Western and Western Christians are increasingly participating on the basis of equality.

The Growing Power of the Nation State

The new age is marked by the enhanced power of the state and the progressive subordination to it of the individual. This trend is seen most strikingly in countries under totalitarian governments. It is also apparent in lands where something of the freedom that characterized nineteenth-century democracy survives. The progress of socialism in Great Britain and western Europe, with the increase there and in the United States of government control, is one of the most familiar movements of our day.

This growing power of the state is closely allied with nationalism. The state professes to be the bulwark of the nation and to be inseparable from it. Patriotism is praised as the major virtue. Loyalty to the nation is tacitly or openly held to take precedence over loyalty to God. The individual is regarded as existing for the sake of what is termed the commonweal, and that commonweal is identified with the nation state.

Here, obviously, is a major threat to what the Christian holds to be the true nature of man and man's primary allegiance. Yet through collective action by the state, if it is rightly employed, can come the furthering of interests with which the Christian is properly concerned — such as adequate food and clothing for himself and others.

Suffering and Uncertainty and the Search for Security

Two of the most widely spread features of the tomorrow that is here are suffering and uncertainty and the search for security.

Never has the sheer mass of physical distress been as mountainous as today. Always mankind has known suffering. Always man has faced hunger, cold, heat, and disease. Only the privileged minority have been able to procure sufficient food, clothing, and housing. Even they have not escaped illness and death. Thanks to the machines and the science that the Occident has developed in the nineteenth and twentieth centuries, millions in western Europe, the British Isles, the United States, Canada, and Australasia have attained a higher standard of physical comfort than the human race has heretofore known. Yet in tragic paradox, more millions are starving or are near starvation today than at any other time in history.

This suffering is the direct result of two things — war and the recent vast increases in population, but in its most acute aspects it is largely a result of World War II. The exhausting concentration of effort on war and the destruction wrought by it have brought want to untold millions in most of Europe and Asia. Only a few countries, notably the United States and Canada, are islands of prosperity in this sea of postwar want. Famine and near-famine stalk abroad in Germany, in Austria, in Italy, in much of the region east of the "iron curtain," in large segments of India, and in many parts of China. Japan is desperately undernourished. Millions of displaced persons are among the major tragedies that are the aftermath of the recent war. These include not only those with whom we are vaguely familiar in Europe but other millions as well, probably more numerous, in China and Japan.

The situation is aggravated by a long-term growth in population. A century and a half ago the total of the inhabitants of the globe is said to have been about 850,000,000. It is now estimated to be approximately 2,200,000,000. This is an increase of about 260 per cent. Much of this increase has been in the relatively vacant lands of the Americas, but a large proportion of it has been in western Europe, where it has come as a result of the industrialization and the nineteenth-century prosperity of that region. Much of it, too, has been in India, Japan, and Java, all of which seemed to have reached the saturation point a hundred years ago. Accurate figures are not obtainable for China, but a vast increase in the birth rate of that land in the relatively peaceful eighteenth century brought the population to a total that the internal discords of the past century and a half, and especially the past fifty years, have apparently not reduced, although it has been maintained with incredible misery to untold millions.

If peaceful economic cooperation among the peoples of the world could be achieved, this persistent growth in numbers would not be an insurmountable obstacle to a general rise in the level of prosperity. In a world such as the one that is here, with its accentuated international, interracial, and ideological tensions, such growth augments the already dangerous friction and so helps to create a vicious circle in which war and the threat of war aggravate suffering, and suffering and the fear of suffering augment the threat of war. Recovery from the destitution wrought by World War II, even if that could be complete, would not remove the menace of this prolonged multiplication of the volume of mankind.

Partly because of this widespread suffering, the unlikelihood of its early or even ultimate complete elimination, and the possibility of its intensification and spread through increased friction, both domestic and international, an air of uncertainty prevails over much of the planet. It is striking in western Europe and Great Britain, where the specter of unaccustomed poverty is ever present, and the competition between Washington and Moscow seems to render erstwhile major powers helpless pawns in the struggle between the two colossi. The friction is also grave in India, where autonomy means division, riots, and possible civil war. It is tragic in China, where inflation and continued war between the National Government and the communists cause further weakness and impoverishment and the prospect of unrelieved gloom for many years to come. Even the United States, powerful and remote from the privations of Europe and Asia, does not feel secure. Its armaments are larger than those during any previous time of peace, and influential elements of the population and the government clamor loudly that they must be even greater.

This suffering and uncertainty, unequaled in their extent, are paralleled by a widespread passion for security. It is partly for this reason that men are willing to acquiesce in the enhanced power of the state. They look to the government for insurance against unemployment, for assurance of remunerative work, for protection against foreign and domestic foes, for care in sickness, and for provision during old age. This demand for security is no less insistent in the more prosperous lands than in the countries where want is clamant.

Overstrain and Weariness

Much of the world shows the effect of the long physical, nervous, and spiritual strain of the war. Sometimes the comparison is made with convalescence from a long illness. The powers of the body have been mobilized to combat the infection. When the disease has been conquered, the body is exhausted and time is required for full recuperation. The parallel is not exact, but it has in it much of truth. A large part of mankind was absorbed in World War II. Each side was straining every effort to win. Men and women were working long hours, were keyed up for endurance, and were giving beyond their normal strength to the demands of the war machine. They were buoyed up by the hope of victory or nerved by the desperate fear of what defeat would mean. The end of the war, they assumed, would at least bring relief. Many believed that victory would usher in a halcyon era. They find that the end of the shooting war has left a legacy of problems greater and more complex than those besetting them on the eve of the conflict.

The vanquished are prostrate. Both Germany and Japan are occupied by their recent foes, and their populations are in dire physical want. Foreign troops are still on the soil of Italy, and that unhappy land, poor before the war, has sounded new depths of misery.

In many respects some of the ostensible victors are no better off. The Chinese had looked forward to what they called reconstruction as though it were a golden age. They find that the tomorrow that is here is one of even greater privation than were the war years, and that the future now appears more bleak than the present. France is distraught by internal dissensions and domestic instability. In much of her colonial empire she faces unrest that she is attempting to curb by costly military action and further drain on her already overdrawn reserves. Great Britain, most of her overseas investments spent in the struggle to win the war, now a debtor rather than a creditor nation, and under the hard necessity of curbing an already limited domestic consumption to bring her exports above the level of her imports, faces her long, uphill haul with grim determination but with worn-out machinery and a tired population. In the United States there is rising resentment at the overseas burdens entailed by the unaccustomed role of continuing commitments in Europe and the Far East. Too little is known of the details of the current Russian scene to give a clear picture of what is happening there, but it is certain that the incalculable loss of property and life caused by the German invasion, and general war fatigue, impede the urgent rebuilding.

An Age of Contrasting Harshness and Kindness

The tomorrow that is here is harsh and cruel, and yet it is marked by relief on an unprecedented scale.

The harshness is all too apparent. War is always accompanied by cruelty and a decay in morals. It was to be expected that a conflict as gigantic as World War II would bring, to a degree heretofore unknown, inhumanity and the abandonment of moral standards. That this has happened is all too clear. Vast concentration camps with their unspeakable cruelties, the virtual enslavement of millions of prisoners of war, rape on a sickening scale in both Orient and Occident, the chronic disregard of sex controls, the deception and murder that accompanied resistance in occupied lands, dishonesty and corruption in private and governmental circles and in the armed services, and the ruthless exploitation of conquered or reconquered areas, whether by the Japanese in China, the Chinese in Formosa, or the Russians in much of Central Europe, are instances all too familiar.

Yet relief has been given in proportions that for magnitude are without precedent. It has come through nongovernmental agencies. It has come through churches and such church-related agencies as the American Friends Service Committee and Church World Service. Scores of committees for the relief of specific peoples have obtained vast sums in the form of hundreds of thousands of voluntary gifts. Much has passed from individual to individual, often at the cost of extreme sacrifice, without the initiative or mediation of any organization. Still larger sums, astronomical in their totals, have been contributed by governments. Much of this financial aid has come through UNRRA; much has come directly from single governments and their civilian and armed representatives.

Partly because of its larger physical reserves the United States has been the source of the major part of these funds. However, the United States and the Americans have by no means been the only givers. Substantial amounts have come from other countries and peoples, and with far greater sacrifice.

A very substantial proportion, perhaps the larger part of the relief, particularly that by governments, has been from prudential rather than unselfish motives. For its own security, the United States has believed help to be necessary for its former enemies as well as for several of its recent allies. Yet in some of

the relief the altruistic motive has been unquestionably dominant. It has also been a factor even in that given by governments.

Racial and Communal Tension and Conflict

The tomorrow that is here is an age of tensions between racial
and cultural groups. The discrimination against Negroes practised by whites in the United States has long been chronic.
Unhappily, the tensions in South Africa have been even more
acute — between Bantu and white, Indian and white, and
Boer and Briton. One of the major tragedies of the day is the
way in which the ancient anti-Jewish feeling has been aggravated
and, because of it, unimaginable cruelties perpetrated. It is
estimated that in the past ten or twelve years one-third of the
Jews of the world have been exterminated. Although the Nazi
campaign for the elimination of the Jews has been ended by the
crushing of Hitler and his party, anti-Jewish feeling remains.
In some areas, including the United States, it is probably increasing. The intensification of the Arab-Jewish conflict in
Palestine is one of the more spectacular features of an uneasy
world. In India, Hindu-Moslem relations, long smoldering, are
in open conflagration. Although in some places the restrictions
placed by Hindu caste on the depressed classes have been
lightened, in other places they are rigidly held to. The wartime
treatment of Japanese in the United States and Canada is a
recent unhappy memory. The persecuting intolerance of communists toward potential or active opposition, the anti-Protes-
tant measures of Roman Catholics in several countries where the
latter are dominant, and the vigorous efforts of Moslems to
curb Christian minorities in Egypt are phases of the same
unlovely intolerance of our day.

Here and there progress has been made toward relieving injustices between groups. This, in general, is true of the treatment of Negroes in the United States. Examples, too, are numerous of Christians who have risked their lives to save Jews from death. Yet, unfortunately, these are merely exceptions to the general trend.

War and Efforts to Curb War

This generation has known the most widely devastating wars in history. It has also seen the most ambitious organized efforts in man's career to eliminate war and to bring order and even-handed justice into relations between nations. World War I and World War II successively involved in active fighting a larger proportion of the earth's population than had any earlier wars. The League of Nations and now the United Nations have brought together the majority of mankind in structures that have given opportunity not only for the peaceable settlement of disputes but for the cooperation of the nations in furthering various aspects of human welfare.

In the tomorrow that is here friction between nations remains. Indeed, tension and the occasion for a major war among the great powers are probably greater than they were on the eve of either World War I or World War II. War weariness and the vivid realization of what renewed war would mean are the chief deterrents and insure a breathing space in which to make potent the machinery for peace.

In this tomorrow, mankind, doubtful and even cynical because of the apparent failure of the League of Nations, is, with wistful and tempered hopefulness, venturing on the United Nations. Through the United Nations, the governments, pressed by the urgency of time, are hesitatingly and fumblingly attempting to devise and agree on some method for controlling atomic energy and for eliminating the lethal weapons that it has made possible. With his ingenuity man has developed processes that can, if misdirected, destroy his flimsy civilization and sweep him off the earth. From the standpoint of geologic time and even of man's course on the planet, civilization is a very recent development. It is obviously imperfect and frail. Man releases the energies of nature far more quickly and easily than he learns to handle himself. Terrified scientists, appalled by the prospect of the destruction that their discoveries can wreak, urge mankind to find a way to forfend disaster, while mankind's leaders seek means of global social control.

The Decay and Growth of Religions

Mankind is ill. The more thoughtful of the race realize that the strains of our time are symptoms of a malady that is inherent in the very constitution of man. Through the centuries man has been seeking a cure for this illness. Sometimes he has attempted to cure it by means of government. Often he has sought a cure in religion. Latterly he has sought healing through programs for the reorganization of state and society on the basis of philosophies that we sometimes term ideologies and that have in them basic conceptions of man and of the universe that are closely akin to religion.

Always, too, there are the eternal questions that man asks about his own nature and destiny, about the strange and poignant struggle that he knows within himself, about the contrast between his frailty and his aspiration for immortality, and about the enigma of the meaning of his existence.

The tomorrow that is here is a mixture of the decay of old religions to which man has looked for the answer to his enigma, the emergence of new faiths and of irreligious secularism, the stubborn resistance of some religions, and the amazing world-wide growth of Christianity.

The present century has witnessed the decline of Confucianism, the system by which a fifth of the human race governed its life. It has seen the forcible abandonment of the state sponsorship of Shinto. In some lands, notably Ceylon and Siam, Buddhism, long stagnant and slowly declining, has been reinforced by a nationalism that elevates it as a political and cultural bond.

As we have earlier suggested, the real religion of a large proportion of mankind is nationalism. Nationalism has had a phenomenal growth in the present century. In the tomorrow that is on us it is increasing. In Russia, it is combined with communism in an intense faith with crusading qualities. In Arab lands, notably Egypt, it takes Islam as a symbol and intensifies that historic religion.

Just now communism seems rampant. This is partly because of its novelty, its promises, and the misery of mankind that leads many persons to clutch at it as at a new Messiah, and partly because of its skillful propaganda.

What we have called secularism is prevalent in many lands and among many groups, both educated and uneducated. In general it affirms that the good things of life are purely of this world, that religion is irrelevant, ineffective, and even hampering, and that to obtain what he desires, man must depend on his own efforts and the scientific processes that he has created.

In contradiction to these many trends is the phenomenal

growth of Christianity. In some areas numerical losses have been encountered, but as a global movement Christianity is showing striking gains. Here is a faith, many centuries old, that in contrast to other long-existant religions is growing apace.

Our Fluid and Urgent World

The age of which we are part is fluid and urgent. The widespread revolution and the accompanying breakup of the old order have put the world in flux. Mankind as a whole can be shaped as never before. Will the growing world church rise to the challenge? Partly because the age is in flux, the situation will not permit delay. In great lands, notably China and Japan, where groping peoples are singularly open to the Gospel, the doors may begin to swing shut within a decade. In India, the depressed classes, among whom the church has made its chief gains, may move toward Islam or Hinduism, or both. In Africa south of the Sahara, the rapid disintegration of the old structure of life leaves millions adrift to be molded, perhaps for generations to come, by whatever forces can move into the vacuum within the next few years. In the Occident, the center of man's illness, where the familiar and heretofore dominant civilization is passing, the new culture is painfully in birth. Communism is gaining apace.

In this fluid and urgent world the church, now growing, must move forward with accelerated pace. Soon after World War I a prophetic Scot declared: "It is either the evangelization of the world in this generation or the damnation of the world in this generation." Events have proved that he foreshortened history — that he was ahead of his time. His uncompromising alternative may well prove the choice in the tomorrow that is here.

Chapter Two

THE CHURCH OF TOMORROW
IS HERE

IN THIS TIME OF REVOLUTION THE CHRISTIAN CHURCH IS growing. In a day when ancient civilizations are passing, the Christian community, one of the oldest existing associations, is becoming world-wide. In an age of turmoil, when the nations are pulling apart and two world wars have wracked mankind, the universal church is building a fellowship that is above national boundaries and is knitting its members together into a community of memory, of present healing and love, and of hope.

This is the more remarkable since the church has been an integral part of that Western civilization that is now dying. In the tomorrow that is here, as in preceding yesterdays, Christianity is surviving the death of cultures with which it has been intimately associated and, freed from ties that were embarrassing it, is moving out to fresh victories.

A History of Advances Following Recessions

At least three times earlier in its history Christianity has had this experience. It is a significant commonplace of the Christmas story that Jesus was born in the reign of the first Roman emperor, Caesar Augustus. Within its first five centuries Christianity had won the nominal allegiance of the overwhelming majority of the population of the Roman Empire. But the Roman Empire and its culture decayed, and Christianity, now so closely associated with them, seemed doomed. Yet, after a prolonged period of shock, Christianity, recovering, enlarged its boundaries and helped to create a fresh culture, that of Medieval Europe. Medieval Europe in turn died, and the church appeared to share its fatal illness. However, the Christian faith, recovering, broke the bonds of the now moribund culture, burst forth in fresh life in the Reformation, and became a builder of the civilization of Modern Europe. Toward the end of the eighteenth century that civilization passed through a major crisis. A partially new culture emerged, that of the nineteenth century. Again Christianity was threatened, and again, moving out afresh in renewed power, it greatly enlarged its geographic borders and its impact on mankind.

A scholar of our day is interpreting the long drama of human history in terms of "challenge and response." Periodically groups of mankind are confronted by new and difficult conditions. Some groups succumb. Others, rising to the emergency, go on to new achievements. The Christian church is the institution that has most successfully displayed the vitality to meet each major challenge and march on to fresh victories.

The Sweep of the World Church

At Whitby the sweep of the world church was vividly seen. It was made to live partly because of the personnel — of which more in the next chapter — and partly because its work was summarized in reports of the delegates on the church in their respective countries. For three successive days statement followed statement until the churches of the entire globe were discussed. To reproduce all that was said would extend these pages far beyond their proper length. We must, however, attempt to give something of the picture, although in condensed survey.

None of the speakers dodged discouraging aspects or difficulties. If anything, these were stressed. Too many delegates at the conference had seen the inside of prisons and concentration camps to permit evasion. Yet throughout the verbal tour of the globe the total impression these delegates gave was one of urgency and hope. As one of the leaders put it, the dominant note was "expectant evangelism."

Western Europe

Any survey of the church in the tomorrow that is here must begin with what has historically been the heart of "Christendom," the continent of Europe, and must pass on immediately to the British Isles and to lands that have been settled from Europe and Britain, namely, the Americas, Australia, and New Zealand.

On the western portion of the continent of Europe the picture is one of (1) the waning of a region that for four and a half centuries dominated the globe, (2) an environment belligerently or passively hostile to the church, and (3) embattled but vigorous Christian minorities. Western Europe is the seat of the largest of the Christian churches, that which looks to Rome for direction. It is also the home of the Protestant Reformation. Here has been most of the scholarship of the church. Here the great theologies have been developed. Even today theological movements on the continent of Europe profoundly affect the rest of the world. From western Europe, through colonization, came most of the geographic spread of Christianity during the sixteenth, seventeenth, and eighteenth centuries, and from this continent also, many of the Christian missions of the nineteenth and twentieth centuries.

Western Europe, so important in the past four and a half centuries, is now in rapid decline. Partial recovery may be accomplished, but the decline is permanent. It is accompanied by great agony of body and even greater agony of spirit. In Germany hopelessness is dominant, and in former German-occupied lands and even in countries that were neutral during World War II, notably Sweden and Switzerland, although these latter have been prosperous, much of nervous uncertainty is in the air.

If one were to view only one side of the picture, Christianity in western Europe would seem to be sharing in the slow death of that region. The churches have been suffering from a drift toward secularism that began before the two world wars. Although in most of western Europe they were closely connected with the state and membership in them was almost universal, for the majority of the adherents the association was nominal. Indifference and even antagonism were rife. To this long-term condition there were added the distresses of World War II. During the war, as before it, the Nazis placed restrictions on the churches in areas under their control. In Germany some open defections occurred, but these were only of minorities. The overwhelming majority still maintain a formal church connection. In Germany and in parts of some other lands extensive destruction was wrought on church buildings. Because of compulsory service in the armies, many parishes were without pastors and the numbers of those training for the ministry dwindled, in some sections to the vanishing point. Because of the dearth of paper and other factors, Christian literature was greatly reduced. Many church periodicals were discontinued and a famine of Bibles developed and is still only partially relieved. In Switzerland church attendance has fallen off.

This is, fortunately, by no means the entire story. The church in western Europe is more vigorous than it was on the eve of World War II. In numbers and physical resources it is weaker, but in what matters most — its inner spiritual vitality — it is stronger. In their resistance to the Nazis, the churches in Germany and the German-occupied countries displayed unsuspected strength. More than any other group, whether political parties, labor organizations, or universities, they maintained centers of resistance to the Nazi flood. The story of the Confessional Church in Germany is familiar to all.

In the Netherlands, the Reformed Church, in its resistance to the Nazis, found itself and achieved church consciousness and organization as it had not for many generations. The heroic record of the leaders of the Church of Norway is a vivid recent memory. In their opposition to the Nazis the churches there won the respect of many who had heretofore disregarded or even despised them. More significantly, many of their members discovered unsuspected resources in their Christian faith and lived more deeply into the meaning of the Gospel than ever.

As for the neutral countries of Switzerland and Sweden, notable theological activity, associated for outsiders with the names of Barth, Brunner, and Nygren, has been maintained. In its relief activities the French Christian CIMADE has been a memorable example of unselfish service in the face of great handicaps. In some parts of Europe, thousands seeking security and the meaning of life in the face of the ruin about them are singularly open to the Gospel. In Germany, the Netherlands, Finland, and Norway, in spite of the distresses of the times, active interest in missions has been maintained. The giving of money has continued, and in some countries, notably in Germany, those wishing to devote their lives to missions outstrip the facilities for training or sending them. On the eve of World War II, German missionaries totaled more than 1,500. Germans now in active missionary service have been reduced to about 400. Of these, many were in British, Dutch, or other enemy territory and were either interned or repatriated. Yet hundreds of German youths, undiscouraged, are offering themselves. From the suffering churches of western Europe fresh streams of life may issue and contribute to the renewal of the churches in more prosperous lands.

Central and Eastern Europe

Eastern Europe — especially Russia — is the stronghold of communism, the center of communist power. It is also the historic home of the family of Orthodox churches. The strongest member of that family is in Russia.

Communism as an idealistic system for reorganizing society has great appeal for many the world over. To those who have lost belief in God it offers a faith and promises a society in which class and racial discriminations, injustice, and poverty shall be removed. By a strange accident of history, in the turmoil that followed World War I communism obtained power in Russia. There it fell heir to the tradition of an absolute police state, that of the czars, and has built up a regime that regiments the individual even more uncompromisingly than did that of the czars. In Russia communism has combined with nationalism and with an earlier tradition of autocratic ambition to build an expanding empire more extensive than that which acknowledged the czars. But more effectively than the czars, it is bringing all the Slavs under its control and by propaganda is creating friendly enclaves in other lands.

In Russia and Central Europe communism has, at least for the moment, made its peace with the Orthodox Church. Communism, it need hardly be said, is basically and officially anti-Christian. The communist believes that religion is "the opiate of the people." In its early years in Russia, the communist regime mingled limited toleration with a kind of persecution, on the theory that the church, deprived of the support of the czarist state, would die out. Latterly, for a variety of reasons, it has become more lenient. Christianity in Russia is far from dead. The Russian Orthodox Church has been allowed more freedom. Throngs attend its services. Evangelical groups are growing. Thousands of Russians outside their native land are accessible to the Gospel; some who have been reached are filtering back into Russia, and are a possible means of strengthening Christianity there. In communist-dominated Bulgaria and Yugoslavia the Orthodox Church has been disestablished. Thrown on its own resources, it may gain in inward vigor. Yet the communist peace with the church is little more than a truce. The fundamental, irreconcilable contradictions persist.

In Greece, in the hour of the nation's sorrow, the Orthodox Church has shown fresh vigor. Movements of laity and clergy seek to give better religious education to youth and to apply the Christian faith to various aspects of life.

The British Isles

How fares the church in the British Isles in the tomorrow that is here? The question is fateful for Protestant Christianity. In the nineteenth and twentieth centuries the English-speaking peoples have been the main sources of the funds and personnel for the Protestant missionary enterprise. Now that Europe is so badly weakened, the weight of providing the physical means for the world-wide church must increasingly fall on them.

Great Britain displays, although to a less extent, the same general conditions that are to be found on the adjacent continent. She has suffered terribly from the drain of the two world wars, and especially from World War II. While her churches have given liberally to missions, they cannot provide the funds to keep pace with the growing costs that accompany the rising price level throughout the world. They must, moreover, rebuild church structures that were destroyed during the war and erect new ones to care for shifting populations. In the past twenty years church membership and church attendance seem to have fallen off. It is said that only from 10 to 15 per cent of the population are closely linked with a church. Much of the population of Britain, like that of Europe, is essentially pagan and is itself a mission field. Only 10 per cent are said to be actually hostile, but 50 per cent are said to be indifferent. The leaders of the British churches are fully aware of the problems that confront them. At the core of the churches are profound conviction and sound life. After the hiatus of the war years, candidates are again coming forward for the ministry at home and for foreign missionary service. Here and there are notable converts from among the intelligentsia. As in the nineteenth century the defection of the intelligentsia preceded that of the masses, so now the conversions among them may be the precursors of a swing to the Christian faith among the rank and file of the population. In Scotland the Iona movement is a symbol of new life.

Canada, Australia, and New Zealand

The three great dominions, members of the British Commonwealth, Canada, Australia, and New Zealand, are collectively large in area but sparse in population. In them, notably in Canada, vigor of church life is maintained, and the overwhelming majority of the population profess some church affiliation or at least some church preference. The churches of Canada especially are sharing substantially in the world-wide Christian enterprise. Those of Australia and New Zealand, as is natural, direct their missionary efforts mainly to the islands of the South Pacific.

The United States

Because of the weakening of western Europe and Great Britain and the small populations of Canada, Australia, and New Zealand, an increasing share of the personnel and funds of the Protestant missionary enterprise must come from the United States.

In the United States a mounting proportion of the population are members of churches. It is estimated that in 1850 only 15.5 per cent of the population were church members. In 1900, the percentage had risen to 35.7, and in 1910, to 43.5. At present, well over 50 per cent of the population have a church membership. Protestants are gaining more rapidly than are Roman Catholics. The Methodist Church reports that in 1946 it added more than 1,000,000 members, and that of these at least 300,000 were on profession of faith, and hence fresh conversions. It seems probable that as the percentage of the population who are church members rises, the degree of religious literacy decreases proportionately and the distinction between the church and the world tends to be blurred. However, many evidences of vigorous religious life are seen. As yet they affect only minorities, but they are varied and are to be encountered in many sections of the country and among widely different groups.

Part of the problem of the urgent tomorrow that is here concerns the lifting of the horizons of the churches of the United States beyond the borders of their own broad land. Christians of the United States are giving millions for overseas relief and for rebuilding the fabric of missions. Hundreds of their youth are offering for service in the world mission. Yet hundreds of millions of dollars are being allocated to new and enlarged church buildings at home, and the majority of theological students never give serious thought to the possibility of spending their lives outside the country. In spite of the enormous responsibilities that the tomorrow that is here is forcing on the United States, the Christians of the land are only beginning to awake to the implications for themselves and their churches.

Latin America

The huge area that is designated Latin America presents a wide variety of peoples and cultures. It has a Latin background. Portuguese is the prevailing tongue in Brazil; Spanish elsewhere. Yet in South America alone Latin America is divided into ten countries, each with its distinctive problems and characteristics; and Central America and the Caribbean contain as many more.

In spite of a history longer than that of the United States, Latin America has an air of youth. Violent ferment is working. The new movements in Europe are having repercussions. The commotion of two world wars and the example of Russia have made for stirrings in the laboring classes.

Conditions vary from country to country. In this report there is room for only broad generalizations and a few specific instances. Traditionally Latin America is Roman Catholic, but for the majority of the people the connection with that church is either very slight or nonexistent. The Roman Catholic Church claims the region as its own and in most countries, in an effort to make itself secure, enters actively into politics. Usually, too, it is allied with landed and other vested interests that seek to maintain themselves against the demands of the masses and find support in the church. The Roman Catholic Church in Latin America is woefully deficient in clergy, both in numbers and in quality. To give even the minimum of pastoral oversight to its flock it should have at least three times the number of priests that now serve it, and the character of many of those it has leaves a great deal to be desired. For these and other reasons the church displays much of corruption, and thousands of the masses and of the high-minded, intelligent folk will have nothing to do with it. If these groups are to be reached by the Gospel, it must be through Protestantism.

Protestantism, or, as it is preferably termed, Evangelical Christianity, is represented in every country and is growing. Its numerical strength varies from republic to republic. It is strongest in Brazil and next strongest in Mexico. Recently Mexico has been the scene of persecution of Evangelicals that has been fomented by the Roman Catholic clergy. Through much of

Latin America local leadership is emerging and Evangelical Christianity is becoming rooted in the soil.

The British West Indies

Geographically near to parts of Latin America are the British West Indies. They occupy only a small fragment of the surface of the earth and contain a minor fraction of the world's population. This population is overwhelmingly Negro. Partly because of a background of slavery and partly because of economic conditions, the family tie is usually lightly held and illegitimacy is high. Yet the people are church conscious, and church attendance, while falling, is large. The majority are Protestants. A dearth of adequate leadership is noted.

Islands of the Pacific

One of the greatest triumphs of the Gospel in the nineteenth and the fore part of the present century was in the islands of the Pacific. Practically the entire population of several of the groups of islands, among them Samoa and Fiji, was won to the Christian faith, and under the influence of the Gospel collective and individual life was made over. In Fiji the influx of thousands of laborers from India later brought in a large non-Christian element, but the original Fijians hold to their Christian faith. On some of the islands the churches are entirely self-supporting and even pay the salaries of the missionaries who serve them. Pacific Islanders have gone as missionaries to other islands, often far distant, there to share in carrying out the Great Commission. At present more young people are offering for missions, notably from Samoa and Fiji, than can be sent. On several of the larger islands, such as the Solomons and New Guinea, where the Gospel has not yet fully penetrated, it continues to make progress.

World War II brought martyrdom to some Christians. Some were exposed to thousands of soldiers and this made for moral deterioration among numerous islanders. Yet many of the most thrilling stories of World War II are those of white soldiers who were profoundly moved by what they saw, through personal contacts on these islands, of the power of the Gospel. Some were converted, and at least one American is going into the Christian ministry because of the impression made on him by a New Hebridean pastor.

World War II also gave to the Christians of the Pacific islands a sense of belonging to the world church. Chaplains and other Christians among the white armed forces brought them in touch with the wider outreach of the Christian fellowship.

Indonesia

At the outbreak of World War II most of the East Indies — which we are now learning to call Indonesia — were under the Netherlands. A vast area, embracing hundreds of islands, large and small, more than half of its population was on the densely settled island of Java, overwhelmingly Moslem by religion. Christianity was making rapid strides, especially among the animistic peoples outside Java. In 1940, there were more Protestant Christians in Indonesia than in all the rest of the Far East. A large proportion of these peoples belonged to what was known as the Protestant Church of the Netherlands Indies. This had been a state church; by 1940, although the separation of church and state had been effected, some remnants of the connection remained. This church was especially strong in the islands north and east of Java, notably in Celebes, and in the northern peninsula of that island, Minahassa. Other groups of Christians had risen through the work of missionary societies, mostly Dutch and German. Notable among these was the church among the Bataks of Sumatra, the outgrowth of German missionary effort. From 1925 on, the Batak Church had been largely independent of control by missionaries. Indonesia also had many Roman Catholics, but they were only about a fourth as numerous as Protestants. Before the war a nationalistic movement had been in progress, but it was limited largely to non-Christians. Christians were not politically minded and were often regarded by their non-Christian neighbors as auxiliaries of Dutch imperialism.

World War II brought striking changes. First came the German occupation of the Netherlands (1940) and the cutting off of the missionaries from their home constituencies. Aid came to the missionaries, partly from local sources and partly through the intervention of the International Missionary Council. Then followed the sudden Japanese irruption. Japanese propaganda helped to promote nationalism and a desire to be free from the Netherlands. True, the Japanese did not grant religious liberty, but by interning the missionaries, they threw the Indonesian Christians on their own resources. Many Christian leaders perished. The Japanese power collapsed as abruptly as it had come.

After its demise, movements arose that issued in the formation of the Indonesian Republic. In Java, the revolt, in its initial stages, contained fanatically Moslem elements and was in part anti-Christian. Since Java has only a few Christians, martyrdoms were few. Through much of Indonesia Christians have become politically conscious and stand for independence. Christians are proportionately more prominent than their numbers would warrant. For instance, the Prime Minister of the Indonesian Republic is a Christian, as was the Commander-in-Chief of the Republican armies. The churches, already thrown on their own resources by the internment of missionaries, have assumed responsibility for self-support and self-direction. Church life is stronger than it was before the war. There are movements to bring the Christians of the widely flung islands into self-conscious fellowship. The Batak Church, now wholly independent, has projects for missions to Moslems. As in so much of the world, there is a dearth of trained leadership. However, steps are being taken to remedy this lack by creating or strengthening training schools. The missionary agencies in the Netherlands favor Indonesian autonomy, both political and ecclesiastical, and, in turn, Indonesian Christians have made it clear that they are eager for missionaries, provided only that they will come prepared to accept the new conditions. Two-thirds of the missionary staff was lost because of the war, but Holland has a large supply of candidates. The atmosphere in the Indonesian churches is one of hope. Numerical gains continue to be made. Some of these, interestingly enough, are in the island of Bali, which is predominantly Hindu in religion and which under the Dutch regime was almost closed to missions. The Batak Church has increased by 50,000 since the outbreak of World War II.

Malaya

The Malay Peninsula, closely related in language and race to much of Indonesia, has been largely under British rule. On the eve of the Japanese occupation the main elements of the population were Malays, Moslem by religion; Chinese, about equal to the Malays in number; and Indians, a smaller group. Almost no missions were conducted among the Malays. The only Moslems who came in contact with Christianity did so through mission schools, and most of the Moslems in these schools were Indians. The Christians were among the Chinese and Indians.

During World War II and the Japanese occupation the church suffered but came through triumphantly, with an increase in self-support. One hundred and fifty lepers were baptized. The greater degree of autonomy granted by the British in the postwar period will make missions among the Moslem Malays even more difficult than before, but among the other elements in the population the church will persist and grow.

The Philippines

The Philippines suffered as severely from World War II as did any land. Destruction of property and life was appalling. The deterioration of morals was marked. Children saw their elders committing acts of dishonesty and violence that in normal times would have been condemned, and they therefore grew up with a weakened sense of right and wrong.

Then came political independence and the necessary adjustments to that new status. It is said that 80 per cent of the church buildings were destroyed. There was a dearth of Christian literature, and four years elapsed without the distribution of Bibles. Copies of the Bible became rare. Yet the Evangelical churches went on. Church services were maintained, with the use of passages that the Christians had memorized. Hundreds were baptized. One reporter at Whitby declared that a religious revival is in progress in the Philippines that is greater than anything that has ever been known there. Churches are being rebuilt and schools reopened. A wider unity among the Evangelical forces is being achieved. Converts continue to be won from the nominal Roman Catholics who constitute the large majority of the population. The Evangelical movement, not yet a half-century old, is flourishing. It needs to replenish its leaders, for many were killed or died of disease. Its three theological seminaries must be strengthened. Yet the outlook is promising.

Japan

The general situation that the church confronts in Japan is one of tragic abnormality. In most of the large cities the destruction by war bombings was prodigious. The Japanese are suffering from shock and extreme war fatigue. From at least September, 1931, they had been the victims of a war psychology, and increasingly after July, 1937, they were under the pressure of large-scale war, with war propaganda, growing privation, and loss of life. Then, in August, 1945, came the collapse, for which they were unprepared, and the utterly unprecedented experience of having their land occupied by foreign troops and directed by foreign rulers. They are suffering from undernourishment, inflation, deprivation of foreign markets, the prostration of industry, and the uncertainty of reparations and of the eventual terms of the treaties that will emerge from the peace. While they are permitted to have their own government, they know that the ultimate decisions must depend not on it but on the conqueror. Yet, by a kind of anomaly, the Japanese have a sense of liberation. They are freed from the dream and the burden of empire and from the kind of regimentation imposed by the state during the war. There are few suicides and there is some measure of humility, and also much vitality and dignity. Religiously, a partial vacuum has been created. Shinto has been disestablished and its state shrines dismantled. It is said that only 10 per cent of the people now go to such shrines as remain. There are bewilderment, apathy, and a loss of sense of direction.

In many respects the church in Japan has suffered. During the war, in the main, it supported the nation. Consequently its message and witness were warped. Relations with the world Christian fellowship were suspended. At least half of the physical plants of the churches and Christian schools are gone. Pastors are either without salaries or with pitifully small ones. Laymen are out of work and can contribute little to the support of the churches.

Yet in some respects the church in Japan is stronger than ever before. It belongs to Japan to a degree that it never belonged in earlier times. Always it had appeared alien. By sharing in the sufferings of the nation during the war, the Christians won acceptance by their fellow Japanese. Katayama, the premier of Japan, is an earnest Christian, an elder in a church. Kagawa, although a third lighter in weight than before the war, nearly blind, and with only one lung, is continuing his evangelism on an enlarged scale. He declares that he gets what he has from God — and that it is not so much strength as fire.

The church in Japan is facing many urgent tasks. It must rebuild its church fabric, regather its members, and restudy and replan its program. Its leadership is aging and it must recruit and train successors. Although it numbers less than one-half of 1 per cent of the population, it must seek to apply the Evangel to all society, and must reach both the cities, with their laboring and commercial classes, and the rural districts. It must further develop the Church of Christ in Japan, the inclusive body that was formed a few months before Pearl Harbor and that embraces nine-tenths of the Protestant Christians of the land. It must renew its contacts with the international Christian fellowship. Hundreds of missionaries from abroad are needed, and needed as soon as they can be sent.

Korea

For forty years Korea was controlled by Japan and under the scrutiny of the Japanese police. During the latter part of that period she was even more strictly regimented, and endured fully as great hardships as the Japanese, except that her cities were not bombed. Now, after the Japanese defeat, divided between the Russians and the Americans, with the prospect of a united independent government indefinitely remote, Korea deserves the sympathy of the world.

The Protestant churches, strong and vigorously evangelistic on the eve of the 1930's, have gone through a decade or more of severe hardship and have emerged loyal to their faith and, although less than 1 per cent of the population, are reaching out actively to proclaim the Gospel to non-Christians. For several years the Japanese attempted to coerce the Christians to participate in ceremonies at the Shinto shrines. Many Christians complied. Scores went to prison rather than conform. At least fifty-six died there. Many pastors were forced into war work, and Sunday services were curtailed. In 1946, missionaries began to return, but they could come only to the American zone. In the Russian zone, where the church is stronger than in the south, the communist authorities have dissolved the Christian youth organizations. They have also arrested some of the pastors. However, church life continues. In Pyengyang, the leading city of the north, fifty churches are going on, the theological seminary has an enrollment of over 250, street evangelistic preaching continues and is attended by throngs, and continuous prayer is being offered in the churches for the relaxation of the communist opposition. In the south, in the American zone, Christian hospitals and schools are being reconstituted. Church services are crowded, in part by Christian refugees from the north.

The urgent needs of the church in Korea are the rehabilitation of the ministry, the increase of the missionary staff, paper for Bibles and other Christian literature, and scholarships for the training of Christian leaders.

China

China is passing through the greatest series of crises in her long history. She has suffered unimaginably. Probably the mass of agony is greater than that of any other people, even the Russians. Years of devastating invasion, a strangling blockade, and now disheartening civil war, all on top of a revolution that for half a century has been sweeping across every phase of China's life — these have taken a fearful toll. It is estimated that China has eighty million homeless and ten million orphans. Fantastic inflation is ever mounting and bringing untold hardship. Moral disintegration is rife. Communism is seeking to enter the vacuum left by the decay of the old culture.

Through these years of agony the church has made progress. To be sure, the majority of missionaries had to leave or were interned; much church property was destroyed; in some places church life was disrupted; and thousands of Chinese Christians joined the exodus from the regions occupied by the Japanese to the west. Under the strain of the war years many of the clergy died. One-half of those who remain are over fifty years of age. New clergy are not being adequately recruited. Christian workers are overweary from the long strain. In communist territory church life is difficult. Leading communists declare that Christianity and communism are incompatible. Yet, while accurate statistics are lacking, the church in China has grown in numbers. The Christians who moved west brought new vigor and breadth of outlook to the churches in that inland area, heretofore remote from the main currents of the world church. In some of the Japanese-occupied cities gains in church membership made good the losses from the westward migration. The fact that Christians shared the distresses of their fellow Chinese and that the churches were centers of relief and hope has given Christianity better standing than it has ever enjoyed. The doors in noncommunist China are open to the Gospel as they have never been. Christians are influential far beyond the 1 per cent that their numerical proportion in the population would indicate. The National Christian Council has projected a three-year Forward Evangelistic Movement. As a feature of that campaign it has as an ideal: every Christian a praying Christian, every Christian a serving Christian, every Christian a witnessing Christian.

Needs are imperative for reaching entire families and Christianizing family life; far too many of the Christians are individuals who have not brought their families with them into the church. Rising costs present grave difficulties to various branches of the church's work, including that of the Christian schools, colleges, and universities. The missionary body, badly depleted during the war, must be enlarged as quickly as possible. More attention should be given to the rural areas, for there dwell at least 80 per cent of the population. As in so many other lands, the recruiting and training of clergy and other Christian workers are clamant needs. All of these problems must be met and solved in the face of as urgent an opportunity as the church has ever known.

Siam

Christians have never been numerous in Siam, for the country is predominantly Buddhist. During the war Christians suffered from petty persecution, and they were threatened with loss of positions in the government or in business if they did not become Buddhists. However, today missionaries are returning, the church is popular, and Christian schools are crowded.

Burma

Christians are more numerous in Burma than in Siam. However, they are predominantly from the non-Burmese animistic minorities, notably the Karens. The Burmese proper are loyally Buddhist and there are only slightly more than five thousand Christians among them.

The war brought great suffering. In some ways the church lost heavily. Spiritually, however, it is today stronger than before the war. During the war Burmese, both Buddhists and Christians, were thrown together intimately in their affliction, and greater appreciation of the Christians followed.

The independence movement that has loomed prominently since the war has absorbed much of the attention of Christians as well as non-Christians. Karen Christians are divided on the issue. In general the older ones distrust independence and the younger ones favor it. Its seems probable that the government of independent Burma will grant religious liberty, not so much from principle as for the purpose of insuring national unity.

Ceylon

In Ceylon, Buddhists are in the large majority and tend to dominate the government as it achieves greater autonomy within the British Commonwealth. Hindus and Moslems constitute large minorities. Christians constitute about 10 per cent of the population, a larger proportion than in any country in South Asia or the Far East except the Philippines. Of the Christians the large majority are Roman Catholics, a community whose strength stems from the period of Portuguese occupation in the sixteenth and seventeenth centuries.

Buddhism is having a revival in Ceylon. This is chiefly on nationalist grounds, for loyalty to the country is held to involve adherence to Buddhism as the national faith. Buddhist nationalism is in part, therefore, anti-Christian, and in one way or another, in part through restrictions on the amount of radio time allowed Christian organizations, in part through discouraging attendance at churches, and in part through impediments to Christian schools, Christianity is being opposed. Opposition is forcing the Protestant forces to come together, and a comprehensive church union is being proposed that will include practically all evangelicals.

India

The church in India has felt the effects of World War II. Although almost no fighting was seen on the soil of India, the country suffered from shortages and rising prices, and Christians and their pastors have shared in the common privations. Thousands of soldiers from other lands were in India. Among these were many Christians who broadened the horizons of the Indian Christians and encouraged them to consider themselves more a part of the world church.

More revolutionary have been the political developments. In August, 1947, two new dominions of the British Commonwealth came into being, Pakistan and India. The ties that bound the native states to Britain as the paramount power were dissolved, and the states had the option of being independent or of joining one or the other of the dominions.

In general Indian Christians have welcomed the new stage in their country's history. They feel that the grounds for the accusation that they are under foreign protection and therefore alien will be removed, and that they will be accepted as authentically Indian. In Pakistan religious liberty may be a problem, for by tradition Moslem states do not permit converts to be won from Islam. The fact that the other dominion is known as India and not Hindustan seems encouraging, for it is an indication that Hinduism will not be regarded by the state as the one religion of the land. Moreover, in the new constitution for India the prospects seem favorable for citizens who wish to change their faith. Thus the continuation of Christian evangelism may be possible. Eventually the Dominion of India will take over the social services, such as medicine and education, in which missions have shared, but for the time being its resources will prove inadequate for the full maintenance of these services, and need and opportunity will exist for Christian participation. Several of the native states have taken measures that will make Christian evangelism difficult.

The outlook for Christianity in India is encouraging. There are already 8 million Christians in the country, or approximately 2 per cent of the population. About half of these Christians are Protestants. Although this Christian population is greater than that of any other land in Asia, there are serious problems. There are, for example, only 3,700 ordained men for 10,000 organized churches and 10,000 unorganized congregations. Yet a spiritual awakening is reported in the churches, especially in rural areas, and much sacrificial giving is in evidence. One Indian leader declared at Whitby that 2,000 additional missionaries are urgently needed to enter the open doors.

The Near East

The Near East presents a varied picture, but in the main only slight progress is being made by the church. Here is the historic center of Islam. Here are the encysted remnants of ancient churches long on the defensive and not reaching out in evangelism among Moslems. Here Islam is the prevailing religion. In Iran, where on nationalistic and not religious grounds mission schools have been closed, a number of Moslems are being won to the Christian faith. In Turkey, a purely secular government places strict regulations on religion. Mission schools can be maintained, but the law forbids religious conversations with students, and any Christian impact must be through the character of the teacher. Yet opportunity is increasing for the distribution of the Bible and other Christian literature. In Syria, although the official religion is Islam, Christians are prominent. In Lebanon, Christians are in the majority, and nationalism is making for cooperation between them and Moslems. In Egypt, nationalism stresses unity and for that reason emphasizes Islam, the religion of the majority. Fairly steady losses to Islam from the Coptic Church, the largest of the Christian bodies, are being seen. Increasingly, discrimination is being practised against Christians in the awarding of employment with the government. The many branches of the Christian church — Coptics, Orthodox, Roman Catholic, and Protestant — are coming together in a common effort for religious liberty. In the vast peninsula of Arabia only a little missionary effort is possible. Yet, in spite of discouragements, in most of the Near East Protestant missions go on and have a decided although unspectacular influence.

Africa South of the Sahara

Some of the most striking gains of the church in the past hundred years have been in Africa south of the Sahara. Here the numerical growth has been phenomenal and the contributions of the Gospel in spiritual and moral transformation have been outstanding. Missions, too, have borne the brunt of reducing languages to writing, of educating the people according to modern methods, and of producing such literature as exists. They have shared with colonial governments in medical care and have been a potent factor in assisting the African to meet constructively the transition forced on him by the coming of the white man and Western civilization.

In the tomorrow that is here vast changes are in progress. Africa is being hurried into the new age. The pace is quickening. World War II brought Africa into closer contact with the outer world than ever before. Thousands of white troops were in Africa, and thousands of black troops were in Europe and Asia. Moreover, even apart from the war, Africa's products are in demand in the markets of the world, and the white man is developing mines and other enterprises to obtain them. The tribal organization continues to disintegrate. The economic and social demands of Africans are increasing. Africans are insisting on more of the physical goods of life. Racial tensions are mounting, and not alone in South Africa. More Africans are being educated in the modern manner and are not content with being subordinate to the whites. The prestige of the white man and trust in him are waning.

To the church and its missionaries this new day brings challenges. The spread of the Gospel and self-support in the churches are making enormous strides. But can the church adequately reach the tens of thousands of laborers who have been brought in to work the white man's mines? Can it make an adequate appeal to the new and growing educated groups? Can rural life, the life of the overwhelming majority, be permeated with the Gospel? The resources of the soil are being wasted through lack of proper agricultural methods. What can the church do about it? Can the church keep pace with the need and the demand for wholesome literature? The education of women and girls is falling behind that of men and boys. This brings problems for the Christian family. Is the church developing a ministry that can give adequate leadership to the new intelligentsia? What can the church do to ease the race tensions? The situation is urgent and will brook no delay.

By Way of Summary

In the maze of details that have been summarized in the preceding paragraphs in what may seem a bewildering fashion, certain general trends stand out. First, as was said at the outset of this chapter, the church is very much alive. Second, in the midst of a hostile world, Christians are a minority. This is no novel experience. From the outset, the world has been hostile to the Gospel, and Christians have been pilgrims and strangers. At times Christians have seemed to forget this. In the western Europe that is now disappearing and even in the United States, church membership has been so much an accepted propriety that the distinction has been blurred and even at times erased. The Occident was being inocculated with a mild form of Christianity in such fashion that it was in danger of becoming immune to the genuine Gospel and its sweeping demands. Now, in Europe, the contrast has again become sharply defined, and loyal minorities are discovering the wealth as well as the uncompromising character of the Gospel. With the aid of missions during the past hundred and fifty years Christian minorities have arisen in practically all lands where they had previously not existed. Some of the minorities are feeble, but in each of them is a nucleus of vigorous life. Third, these minorities are being bound together in a conscious world-wide fellowship. This is the Ecumenical Movement of which we are now, fortunately, hearing so much. Here is a fellowship that was strengthened rather than weakened in the tragic years of World War II. It is growing. In it the church of tomorrow is foreshadowed; to the discerning, it is already here. It was vividly seen at Whitby. In the same month it was finding expression in the World Conference of Christian Youth at Oslo. It is also being seen in the World Council of Churches, still officially in process of formation, but very much alive and expanding. It is being witnessed in other organizations such as the World's Student Christian Federation, the World Council of Christian

Education, formerly known as the World's Sunday School Association, the world organizations of the Young Men's and Young Women's Christian Associations, and in many a local and national body that in one way or another is an expression of the rising urge for Christian unity. In an age of world turmoil, Christianity is ceasing to be Occidental and is becoming in fact what it has long been in principle, world wide. In spite of their many divisions, Christians are drawing together, and on a global scale.

All that we have attempted to say in this chapter was concrete and vibrant at Whitby. It is to a description of the Whitby gathering that we must now turn.

Chapter Three

THE REALITY OF THE FELLOWSHIP

O N THAT FIRST SUNDAY MORNING AT WHITBY THEY WENT to the altar in groups of eight — Christians, missionary folk all. Had a commentator been present, he would with solemn effectiveness have called the roll of the nations and races as each person in that small company of about one hundred and twenty moved forward to participate in the Lord's Supper. The delegates were drawn from around the globe and represented every color of the human race. They had come together from a world of chaos and strife, suffering and despair.

In such a setting it was only a matter of moments before everyone in that plain, sunlit school assembly room, which now served as a sanctuary for worship, felt himself part of a living bond of kinship in Christ. Each knew, as surely as it is given human beings to know, that he was one with every other person present. That group represented the whole community of mankind, and those who experienced their oneness in Christ and the power known in the presence of the spirit of God can never forget the high and holy joy of that hour. The experience was the reality in each life of the fellowship that is given to those who confess Jesus Christ as Lord.

How perfectly the four celebrants of the Holy Communion symbolized the world outreach of the church! All were Anglicans, for this first of several observances of the Lord's Supper was celebrated according to the Anglican rite. Archbishop Mowll of Sydney, Australia, a man who had spent many years of his life in China, had as a fellow-celebrant a Chinese friend, Bishop Robin Chen. And officiating with these two were the Reverend R.O.C. King, a West Indian Negro, and the Reverend Mahmood Rezavi, a first-generation Christian, a Persian convert from Islam. What rich meaning was conveyed in the opening words of the communion prayer: "O God, who hast made of one blood all nations of men . . ."! Here before the eyes of all participants was a symbol of the reality of their fellowship.

And to what a representative group from the world church did these four minister! Bishops and laymen knelt together at the altar to partake of the bread and the wine. John Subhan had come from India. As is true of so many others present, an intensely gripping book could be written of his life. There is space here to record only the bare facts that he was converted from Islam and that he is now a bishop of the Methodist Church. Kneeling with the Indian bishop were the Lutheran Bishop Axel Malmstrom and his wife from Denmark. Mr. Alberto Rembao, the Mexican editor of *La Nueva Democracia;* Mrs. Pao-Chun Nyi, a doctor from Shanghai; and U Ba Hlaing, a lawyer, and now president and chief executive officer of Mandalay Municipality, Burma, were fellow-participants in that communion service. University professors John Baillie of Edinburgh and Knut Westman of Uppsala knelt with the Reverend Christian Baeta from the Gold Coast of Africa and the Reverend Setareki Tuilovoni from the Fiji Islands, striking in appearance because of his great shock of bushy black hair. Count Steven van Randwijck of Holland and the Reverend

Toenggoel Sihombing and the Reverend Wilhelm Johannis
Rumambi of Indonesia communed together, as did the Reverend Emile Schloesing of France and Professor Carl Ihmels
from the Russian-occupied zone of Germany. One could think
only of Paul's lofty description, "Here there cannot be Greek
nor Jew, circumcised and uncircumcised, barbarian, Scythian,
slave, free man, but Christ is all, and in all." The reality of that
living unity in Christ stirred every heart to its depths. It was
more real than the physical surroundings.

Those who communed here recognized this as one of the high
moments of their lives. They knew that the Holy Spirit had
been among them. The thoughts of many were directed to the
occasion of Pentecost and the first great outpouring of the
Spirit. (That thought recurred many times in the days that
were to come.) There had been in that earlier day one hundred
and twenty together "with one accord in one place." It was
those original disciples who had launched the world mission of
the church, and here in like manner were their heirs, assembled
to seek the guidance of the Holy Spirit for the further pur-
suance of the world mission of the church — the church whose
genius since its inception has been that it is missionary. The
same number, the same unity, the same felt presence of the
Spirit, and the same task before them! Had the all-embracing
reality of the oneness with Christians of every age and every
land ever been experienced more deeply?

But what of the larger gathering of which this service of Holy
Communion was a part? It assembled at Whitby, Ontario, in
Canada, from July 5 to July 24, 1947. Popularly designated
"The Whitby Conference," it was an Enlarged Meeting of the
Committee of the International Missionary Council. Such

nomenclature conveys little meaning, however, unless one understands the council's nature and genesis. For what purpose had it brought together these people from around the world? What kind of people were they? And more important, does what they did have any significance for the man in the pew in Manchester, Bombay, Los Angeles, or Nanking?

The International Missionary Council

In a very real sense the International Missionary Council is one of the products of the Evangelical Awakening of the late eighteenth and early nineteenth centuries. Modern Protestant missions are usually considered to have begun with William Carey's going to India, in 1793. Within a short time numerous missionary societies were formed in England, on the continent, and in the United States for the fulfillment of the Great Commission of Jesus Christ. It is only natural, then, that as these missionary societies pursued their similar tasks they should come together in interdenominational conferences to consult with one another and to inform the members of the churches of their work and of their needs.

The first of these interdenominational missionary conferences was convened for two days in New York in 1854. The occasion was the arrival in America of Dr. Alexander Duff, a missionary to India. Another similar conference assembled for four days in Liverpool in 1860. Eighteen years later, in London, nearly 160 persons met together for five days to evaluate the effectiveness of their societies' missionary endeavors. And in 1888 a large world-wide missionary conference was held in London. Of its nearly 1,500 members, 1,341 were British. Largely as a result of this great London gathering, there met in New York for ten days in 1900 the Ecumenical Conference — "Ecumenical" because the conference represented missionary work in every part of the world, not because it represented all branches of the Christian church. Of the 1,500 present, some 600 were foreign missionaries. At the time no provision was made for a succeeding conference, but another was held ten years later, and it proved to be epoch making.

Edinburgh, 1910

The World Missionary Conference of 1910, which met at Edinburgh, stands in the direct succession of the conferences already described, but it marks the real watershed between the loosely related attempts at missionary cooperation that came before it and the more effective organizations that have since developed for cooperative endeavor in the Christian world mission. Both the International Missionary Council and the World Council of Churches [1] stem directly from Edinburgh, and 1910 is therefore frequently referred to as the beginning of the modern Ecumenical Movement. The word "ecumenical," which is gaining wider currency in the churches today, means "as broad as the inhabited world." It refers to world Christianity — Christianity that is world wide and united. The Ecumenical Movement is a trend toward the development of a consciousness in all the churches of the church universal conceived as a world missionary community. Its primary concern is making the Gospel effective the world around, and to this purpose organization is subsidiary.

[1] The World Council of Churches is still technically "in process of formation," although it has been functioning effectively since 1938. Delayed in its official formation by the war, the World Council of Churches will be actually constituted by its first Assembly at Amsterdam in late August, 1948.

Several distinguishing features characterized the World Missionary Conference of 1910. It was the first of the interdenominational missionary conferences the membership of which (1,355) was comprised of delegates appointed officially by missionary societies whose allotments were determined in proportion to their expenditures on the field. It was thus truly representative. Furthermore, it was in the fullest sense a *conference*. Previous missionary gatherings had been built around platform addresses, but as a result of a preliminary two-year study program there was real give and take at Edinburgh, and the conference produced much helpful consultation. Finally, it created a Continuation Committee through which the work of the conference was to be continued and through which the conference would be perpetuated.

The International Missionary Council's Formation, 1921

The Continuation Committee was brought into being on the threshold of World War I, with Dr. John R. Mott as its chairman. Before the outbreak of hostilities in Europe, Dr. Mott traveled around the world to organize bodies that later became national Christian councils. Each national council facilitated cooperative, united endeavor among the churches. However, when the war began, resultant animosities threatened to disrupt the Continuation Committee, but this catastrophe was averted by the establishment of an Emergency Committee in 1918. The new body served especially to safeguard the freedom of French and German missions and was largely instrumental in making possible an important meeting at Crans, Switzerland, in 1920.

At Crans the atmosphere was tense as a result of the strain of misunderstanding arising from the war, but plans emerged for the creation of the International Missionary Council. This organization was constituted one year later, in 1921, at Lake Mohonk, New York, as an international council linking together in one body the national Christian councils and the national missionary conferences of the world in the common task of world evangelization. Thus the International Missionary Council came into being, not as a legislative body, but as an advisory council for its constituent members.

It is obvious, then, that an individual denominational missionary society does not have membership directly in the International Missionary Council. It is represented in that council through its membership in a national organization such as the Foreign Missions Conference of North America (United States and Canada), the National Christian Council of China, or the Conference of Missionary Societies in Great Britain and Ireland. Twenty-six of these national bodies (although some few include more than one nation) comprise the membership of the International Missionary Council.

The Jerusalem Conference, 1928

The first world assembly of the International Missionary Council met in Jerusalem at Easter time, 1928. In some respects the Jerusalem Conference differed markedly from the Edinburgh meeting in 1910. It was a smaller gathering. Delegates numbered only 250. But another contrast was of far greater importance. At Edinburgh 1 per cent of the delegates were nationals from the lands of the younger churches, and they came, not as representatives of their churches, but as part of the quota of the parent missionary societies of the older churches. At

Jerusalem roughly one-fourth of the delegates were nationals from the lands of the younger churches, and they came representing their own national Christian councils. Many of the younger churches were seen to be churches in their own right and with capable leadership. Some were self-supporting and carried on their own missionary work. This shift in qualified representation was, and increasingly is, one of the most important factors to reckon with in world Christianity. Furthermore, for the first time Latin America was represented. And appropriately, too, the Orthodox churches were present. From the conference two new organizational arms for the International Missionary Council emerged: the Department of Social and Economic Research and Counsel, and the Committee on the Christian Approach to the Jews. Both continue today as part of the council.

The Madras Conference, 1938

Considerable progress had been made in the work of the International Missionary Council when it held its next world meeting at Madras, India, at Christmas time, 1938, on the very eve of World War II. Indeed, Hangchow, the site originally chosen for the meeting, had to be abandoned because of the "undeclared" war between Japan and China that had broken out in July, 1937. The final decision whether or not to proceed with the Madras meeting had to be made only a few days after Munich. The period was an extremely trying and ominous one in which to bring together a world conference. But of what portent for the future that, when the nations of the world were pulling apart and preparing for the worst holocaust mankind has known, the most widely representative meeting ever assembled under any auspices met at Madras to outline the program of the Christian world mission in the next terrible years ahead! Four hundred and seventy people, of whom more than half now represented the younger churches, came together at Madras. There they laid such a solid foundation and so closely cemented the ties of the Christian world community that after World War II, the solidarity of that community was preserved intact, as it had not been in the strained period following World War I. Indeed, it was strengthened by the testing of war. This point was made graphic at Whitby.

World War II and Orphaned Missions

During the war the International Missionary Council had many heavy responsibilities. However, its best known and most unusual undertaking was what has come to be known as "Orphaned Missions." The outbreak of the war obviously severed German missions from their base at home. Shortly, too, French, Danish, Norwegian, Finnish, and Dutch missions were similarly "orphaned." Prompt action averted what otherwise would have been a tragedy. A new and thrilling chapter was written in the history of the church. From China, from Mexico and Argentina, from the Congo, from the Straits Settlements, from Syria, from Great Britain and the United States — yes, even from Japan — money was contributed by many denominations for the support of missions that had been cut off from their home source of income. Since November, 1939, well over five and a half million dollars have been contributed to the Orphaned Missions Fund. And so far as is known, as a result of the Fund not a single Protestant missionary anywhere in the world has had to leave his post during the war years because of lack of funds. This amazing story can be recorded only because a world Christian community does exist, and because that community has world-wide organizations such as the International Missionary Council as its functioning arms. The community is a fellowship that knows no barriers of race and nation.

In February, 1946, the *Ad Interim* Committee of the International Missionary Council assembled in Geneva for its first official meeting after the war. Direct contact with many in Europe and elsewhere, impossible during the war, was renewed, and the immediate next steps necessary for further work were taken. In a few weeks it became apparent that while an early representative world meeting would have to be small, it was of the utmost importance. The effects of the war on the world missionary enterprise needed to be assayed and a strategy had to be determined. The spiritual tie of the world fellowship had remained unbroken, but after the years of war an opportunity for Christian missionary leaders to renew their friendships in face-to-face meeting was imperative. Thus was conceived the Whitby Conference of the International Missionary Council.

The Whitby Conference, 1947

When the Whitby delegates assembled, they had before them a threefold purpose: first, to determine how the war had affected the work of the church throughout the world and to measure effectively the gains and losses; second, to "rediscover" the meaning of the old yet ever new Christian Gospel for a devastated, utterly confused, and despairing world; third, in complete dependence on the spirit of God, to seek a plan of action for united effort in the common Divine Commission of the older and younger churches — the winning of mankind to Christ.

The keynote set for Whitby's sessions was evangelism as the one great task of the church in the world today.

Whitby's Setting

Like a sheltered island in a peaceful cove while a storm rages on the sea — this was the quiet little town of Whitby in the summer of 1947. Lying east of Toronto on the shore of Lake Ontario, it seemed remote from all the swirling currents of a world in turmoil. During the three-week course of the Whitby meeting, the Paris Conference on European Economic Cooperation was in session. The New York *Times* on July 20 reported that the close of the Paris sessions made final the economic break between Russia and the West. At the same time tension was mounting in Palestine, with an increasing number of sporadic outbursts of violence. The Dutch began what amounted to a colonial war in Indonesia. China was letting her blood in a ruinous civil war. India was seething, with internecine conflict a grim prospect. Virtually the whole world was in agony. But life in Whitby continued as it had in the past. The town's substantial homes and well kept lawns betokened prosperity and a way of living difficult to discover elsewhere in the world. On the edge of the village unpaved streets overhung with leafy maples gradually merged into fields of newly mown hay and ripening grain. For those who had to return to Holland, to Germany, to Palestine, to India, to China, and to Indonesia, Whitby was a momentary haven in the midst of tragedy and terror — symptoms of revolution already in progress.

The Canadian Overseas Missions Council was the generous host of this meeting of the International Missionary Council. The conference itself met at and enjoyed the gracious hospitality of the Ontario Ladies' College, which looks more like a country estate than a campus. It was, indeed, originally an estate. The one large building of the college, where delegates met and were housed, had been constructed in the mid-nineteenth century. The builder of the Victorian gothic structure had aspired to entertain royalty. He had prepared, without knowing it, a perfect meeting place for this twentieth-century conference.

The campus-estate was ringed with trees that set it apart. Its long, gently sloping lawns held great appeal for old friends who wished to stroll. In the afternoons and evenings little groups assembled under the shade trees to converse and enjoy the gardens or the colorful bed of geraniums and cannas hedged in on the terrace by two ancient cannons that guard the entrance to the college. On this campus-estate Christian delegates from the far corners of the earth lived, met, and played together. The world of revolution from which they had come was uppermost in their minds. Each would return to its strife. But the life of a lived tomorrow was the priceless gift they could take back to that world.

Unity in Diversity

For most of the one hundred and twelve missionary folk from forty nations gathered at Whitby this was the first opportunity since the war to renew acquaintance with colleagues from other lands. And from what divergent backgrounds out of the war years they came! There were those present who had been in prison. Some had been tortured. Others, starving, had stared death in the face. Some had seen loved ones tortured and killed before their eyes. There were those who had chosen the opposite horns of resistance and collaboration in the dilemma that confronts one whose homeland is held by an enemy power. There were others whose homes had been blasted to bits by planes from former enemy countries now represented by persons present as co-workers. Those who remembered the strained nature of similar gatherings after the last war would have been prepared for any tenseness that might have resulted.

What did emerge, however, was beyond all expectation. One must recall that all present were convinced Christians, and prior to the war their nurture had been in the world-wide fellowship of the Ecumenical Movement — the great new fact of today in the Christian church and in a world torn by hate. In the past years each had been praying for those whom, since the desolate blackout of war, he now saw for the first time. For months they had been joined in prayer for the blessing of God on this meeting. Spiritually they had been one. There was no separation of distance now. All were together. This was a reunion of kindred minds and souls. It was like a family, after a disastrous flood, discovering that all its once-scattered members are safely reunited, abundantly grateful to be together again. The living experience of each in oneness with the other in Christ was the supreme reality. The joy of that unity was not lessened but heightened and made even more meaningful because of the rich diversity of nationality, race, and experience. What mattered was that those who knew one Lord and Father were now one in common cause and fellowship. Even the few for whom this was the first ecumenical meeting were caught up into, transformed by, and made a part of this fellowship whose unity and high joy were unique. The all-pervasive sense of God's presence and of a fellowship of shared love for God and for one another in that presence was Whitby's most real experience. Exhilarating, it was at the same time profoundly moving. One who lived in the midst of such realized Christian love could only believe, in faith and quiet assurance, that it was a foretaste of what is to come. It was in that spirit that some-one said, "I feel as though tomorrow has come at last." Indeed, a person who had experienced what was lived at Whitby could say gloriously, "*Tomorrow is here.*"

Over the years there have been other gatherings rich in spiritual unity. But delegates who had attended the major ecumenical conferences of this generation were alike in their judgment that none had equaled the unity and harmony of fellowship that characterized Whitby. Dr. John R. Mott, the only Whitby delegate present at every meeting of the International Missionary Council from Edinburgh on, stated that never in all his experience had he known a gathering of more manifest unity of spirit and purpose.

Whitby and Its Predecessors

In the words of the International Missionary Council's chairman, Bishop James C. Baker of the Methodist Church, Whitby stood in the same succession and was "quite as much a meeting of the International Missionary Council as Jerusalem and Madras." But Whitby differed in several respects from its predecessors. Jerusalem and Madras were both meetings of *the Council*, while Whitby was an enlarged meeting of *the Committee of the Council*. Numerically Whitby was smaller, and, as one would expect, fewer countries were represented. Including regular and fraternal delegates, speakers, officers, consultants, and staff, there were 112 conference members from 40 different countries. Of these members 36 were from the younger churches. Thus with 32 per cent of its constituency from the younger churches, Whitby was more representative of the younger churches than was Jerusalem, but less representative than Madras. If, however, one's percentage is reckoned on the 68 persons representing countries, then Whitby was slightly more representative of the younger churches than Madras. Seven per cent of Whitby's members were women. Proportionally only about one-half as many were present as at Madras. The average age of Whitby's delegates was fifty-two.

The Post-Mott Era

When the conference assembled for its first formal meeting, John R. Mott, who had chaired superbly Edinburgh, Jerusalem, and Madras, no longer sat first in command. This elder states-man of the church, whose hand more than any other had guided the International Missionary Council from its inception, had retired from its chairmanship five years before the Whitby conference. During sixty years of devoted and Herculean service to world Christianity, he had given incomparable leadership in five great ecumenical organizations. But at Whitby, not far from the chair that had once been his, he sat regularly in the front row among the delegates. Since Madras an epoch in the history of modern missions had passed. People spoke now of "the post-Mott era." Deep emotion surged through the con-ference as Dr. Mott, eighty-two, but as in earlier days with keen, piercing eyes deeply recessed beneath bushy eyebrows, stood to deliver the opening address. The assembled missionary leaders arose as a man in tribute, applauding with heartfelt gratitude this giant whose labors were unique.

A World Purview

The initial task of the conference was to gain a comprehensive view of the state of the churches in various countries at the close of the war. The first country to be heard from was Japan, and by common accord the presentation was the most complete and thorough analysis given. But it was made by an American. Dr. Charles W. Iglehart had prepared it at the last minute when it became apparent that the delegate from Japan could not attend. The Japanese who was to have been present had been turned back at the dock in Japan as the result of a decision by the Far Eastern Commission (established, it will be recalled, by the victorious powers). This decision was deeply regretted many times during the conference. The Japanese delegate's coming had been anticipated, because it had the approval of General Douglas MacArthur, commander of the occupying forces in Japan. His absence left Japan the only member country of the Committee of the International Missionary Council not represented at Whitby.

Asia was the first continent surveyed. Bishop W. Y. Chen of the Methodist Church was especially admired by the newsmen for his forthright honesty in describing the situation in his homeland, China. Interestingly enough, the Bishop had never attended a theological seminary. He entered the ministry as a "local preacher," that peculiarly Methodist institution by which a layman is licensed to preach. His ordination to the ministry came some years later. Two capable leaders from Korea, Dr. Kwan Sik Kim and Dr. Fritz Hongkyu Pyen, reported for their country. Delegates quickly appreciated Dr. Pyen's quick mind and cheerful manner, but few knew the story of how he had been tortured, several times almost to death, in a wartime Japanese prison. During his imprisonment no pain had been intense enough to bring him to recant his faith. In fact, the effect of this witness on his jailor combined with other factors to cause the latter first to fear the God of the Christian and then so to admire his prisoner that he released him.

It was a woman, Dr. Josefa Ilano, who reported for the Philippines. In her gay and elaborate native dress, a *mestisa* made of pineapple fiber, she was strikingly attractive. Although petite and demure, she could pour out her heart and move her audience with dynamic force. It was difficult to imagine this small, attractive woman beside an operating table; but she had been a surgeon for twenty years. She had seen her islands invaded and she had witnessed the savage butchery of war. It was even more difficult to picture her following with two loyal friends in the wake of the infamous Bataan "Death March," and until she was forced to flee to the hills, caring for those who fell by the wayside. When Dr. Ilano spoke of an unshakable faith in Christ that no bomb or bayonet could destroy, tears welled up in her eyes, for those same eyes had beheld members of her own family put to death by bomb and bayonet. Her experiences not only tested but deepened her Christian faith. When she returns now to her people, it will not be as a surgeon. Shortly before Dr. Ilano left the Philippines, a crashing tree pinned her to earth and so injured her right side that she can no longer wield a scalpel. She is content to be a practising physician and so continue her twofold ministry to physical and spiritual need.

In the first conference session, when the names of those

present were read, the three German representatives received the only ovation accorded to delegates. That ovation was a symbol of the warm gratitude with which they were welcomed into a fellowship from which their faces had long been absent. As the situation in Germany was surveyed by Dr. Karl Hartenstein, Pralat of Württemberg, persons strained attentively to hear every word. He affirmed that through the past ten years the source of deepest comfort to Christians in Germany was the knowledge that they were part of the ecumenical church. And many were surprised to hear Dr. Walter Freytag, director of the German Evangelical Missionary Council and professor of missions at Hamburg and Kiel, tell how, in a school of suffering and poverty, thousands of young Christian missionary candidates in Germany are being trained for service. One by one the nations were heard from until the three-day world survey was completed.

Women of the Younger Churches

The caliber and ability of the women from the younger churches were most impressive. What eloquent testimony each bore in her own life to the power of the Christian Gospel! It is only regrettable that too few were present to represent adequately the share of women in the world mission of the church. Mention has already been made of Dr. Ilano. She had a colleague from China in Dr. Wang (Mrs. Pao-Chun Nyi). Dr. Wang, who was trained at Johns Hopkins in the United States and who speaks perfect English, is chief gynecologist at Margaret Williamson Hospital in Shanghai, where her husband is a leading surgeon. In addition to practising medicine and doing church work, she has reared a son, who is also studying medicine. Miss

Violetta Cavallero of Uruguay spoke for the Christian women of Latin America. With what eloquent simplicity this young woman reminded the conference that, in any total or effective program of evangelism, it must make adequate provision for the Christian nurture and training of children! Present also was Mrs. Prem Nath Dass of India, president emeritus of Isabella Thoburn College at Lucknow and holder of several doctorates. She was equally at home discussing with churchmen the future of the church in India and sitting on the lawn in the midst of a group of Whitby children telling stories of her native land. One surmised, however, since her own children are now grown, that she preferred the youngsters to the churchmen. In her native saris of brilliant red, yellow, or green, Mrs. Dass was the most colorfully dressed person at Whitby.

Whitby out of Session

What is now the total conference experience took place as much outside the assembly hall as inside. One could sit at the dinner table with Christians of eight nations. Several of the news reporters, enjoying this experience for the first time, were as thrilled as any delegate. One man, on assignment for Reuters and the Associated Press, admitted that he was greatly impressed by the frankness and clear thinking of these missionary folk, and added that any one meal was the equivalent of a semester course in college! Another suggested that the fact that the "hardboiled" press had devoted so much space to the "brotherhood" of Whitby indicated how much real news value the conference had.

Each morning there was coffee, and each afternoon, tea. These periods afforded a mid-session pickup with pleasant conversation.

They also provided the hard-working secretaries and staff momentary relaxation from their duties. Nevertheless, Dr. John W. Decker, the council's New York secretary, and the Reverend Norman Goodall, its London secretary, used most of these occasions for further consultations with their colleagues, Dr. Leland S. Albright of New York, the Reverend Charles W. Ranson of London (who more than any other person was responsible for the preparation of Whitby's program), and the Misses Betty D. Gibson, Doris H. Standley, Margaret Sinclair, and Margaret Wrong of London. No one attending the sessions will forget the modest hesitancy with which Mr. Ranson, a former missionary in India, from his seat at the secretaries' table, would ask the chair for the floor. Tall and able, he spoke with earnest conviction and force. The conference made a happy choice when it elected him to the newly-created post of general secretary of the International Missionary Council.

A Conference in Tomorrow's World

In several ways the conference was part of the tomorrow that is here. Not only are missionaries using the latest equipment in radio for their work, but from Whitby they were heard by the world through that same medium. One major American network carried a half-hour program of the conference. And a service of worship from Whitby was beamed to the world by the British Broadcasting Corporation. Just before air time, the Canadian announcer, impressed by the atmosphere of the meeting, urged that delegates try to send that same spirit over the air. But after a moment's reflection he added, "I know it will carry over. It's so genuine." He had caught it in just a few moments!

The airplane also figured prominently. President H. P. Van Dusen of Union Theological Seminary in New York, who gave outstanding and prophetic leadership at Whitby, and Dr. O. Frederick Nolde, director of the Commission of the Churches on International Affairs (jointly sponsored by the World Council of Churches and the International Missionary Council) had been in Geneva at a committee session of the World Council of Churches in the days immediately prior to Whitby. Transoceanic plane service enabled them to lose only one day between sessions in Geneva and Whitby! Bishop Stephen Neill, assistant to the Archbishop of Canterbury, had been in the same sessions at Geneva. Flying directly to Whitby, he shouldered in the drafting committee the major responsibility for producing and subsequently revising the Whitby report. His two-weeks work completed, he flew to Oslo, Norway, to preach at the final Sunday service of the World Conference of Christian Youth that was meeting simultaneously with Whitby. Certainly the world in which Whitby was set is already living in a technological tomorrow.

The Eternal Gospel

Three days out of the heart of the conference were given to discover afresh the eternal Gospel. The chapter that follows is intended as a fuller interpretation of those days; but here let it be noted that in its consideration of "the Given Word" and in its concern for the articulation of that Word to mankind, the conference enlisted in its service the best minds of the younger and older churches. Dr. John Baillie, of Scotland; Principal David G. Moses, of India; Professor Walter Freytag, of Germany; Professor T. C. Chao, of China; and President H. P.

Van Dusen, of the United States, all contributed. The final sessions of these days centered on the Holy Spirit as "the Dynamic Word," and were conducted by Professor Lootfy Levonian, of Lebanon, and President John Mackay, of the United States.

A New Relationship

To consider the relationship of the younger and older churches as partners in obedience to the Great Commission, members of the younger churches and members of the older churches separated into two groups. An observer would have been thrilled by the meeting of the younger church leaders. From South Africa, from Ceylon, from Siam, from China, from Korea, from the Fijis, from Mexico, Brazil, and Argentina, from Iran and Lebanon, these delegates sat together seeking answers for their shared problems. One would hear in English a Portuguese-speaking Brazilian seek the permission of the floor from the English-speaking Chinese chairman, to answer a question put to him in English by a Tamil-speaking Malayan. The common language here, as for the entire conference, was English. Under the capable chairmanship of the Chinese Anglican, Bishop Robin Chen, was a group assembled from the far corners of the earth pursuing in perfect fashion a democratic discussion. One could not help thinking, as he listened to Mr. Rallia Ram and Dr. Rajah Manikam of India, to Professor Gonzalo Báez-Camargo of Mexico, to the Methodist Bishop W. Y. Chen of China and his chairman-colleague Bishop Robin Chen, to U Ba Hlaing of Burma, and to others, that here were men as capable as one could find anywhere in the world. Certainly their like could not be surpassed in any government council or even in the United Nations.

While the members of the younger churches met to draw up their recommendations, members of the older churches were in similar meeting. The agenda of each group included the same thorny problems: the disparity between payments to missionaries and to national workers; the question whether the missionary's primary responsibility is to the church to which he goes in the field or to the church that sends him; and the role of the giving churches in determining the policy and program of the receiving churches. When the two groups came together to present their reports, many could remember the heated discussions of former years on the same questions.

And then occurred a most remarkable event. First the report of the younger churches was read, then that of the older churches. Except for the preliminary clearance of agenda by the respective chairmen, there had been no consultation whatsoever between the two groups, yet the two reports in their recommendations point for point were virtually identical! The air was electric. There was a momentary pause. Someone spoke briefly of the unique nature of these two reports. And then from the rear of the room, Mrs. Dass of India suggested singing the Doxology. And with what heartfelt gratitude it was poured forth that morning! When it was concluded, Dr. John Mackay, President of Princeton Seminary, arose and spoke slowly: "This has been the work of the Spirit. These two documents are so remarkable that they should be allowed to stand as evidence of what two groups of brethren can achieve when they have been working together in common cause and seeking God's will." This was another high moment (for some the highest) in a conference that moved not to a single climax, but from one lofty peak to another.

No matter how one calculates the representation of the

younger churches, there was a oneness of spirit and outlook on the part of both younger and older churches such as had never before been witnessed. It was freely acknowledged that the terms "older" and "younger" when applied to the churches had lost much of their meaning and that in many respects they were now outmoded. Because the delegates felt this new sense of being yoked together as partners in one great task, the tensions that in the past frequently had resulted between older and younger churches were not in evidence at Whitby. That harmony and solidarity were glorious music to the ears of all. At Whitby "older" and "younger" were one. The prevailing spirit was "one church for the world."

There was not a delegate who did not desperately long for some Aladdin's lamp whose genie he might command to assemble the congregations of all churches and persons outside the churches in his homeland so that they might experience the united, joyous fellowship and deep, courageous hope prevailing at Whitby. Here in very fact, vibrant and alive, was that for which the world is starving. Could others only see and experience, they might know Him through whom came the reality of the fellowship, through whom alone it is possible. How each yearned that all churches of the world could share this fellowship, which was the well remembered prayer in John's Gospel: "That they may all be one; even as thou, Father, art in me, and I in thee, that they also may be in us *so that the world may believe that thou hast sent me.*" For those at Whitby the tomorrow for which mankind longs had already arrived. Then and there they could say, "Tomorrow is here." They had lived in tomorrow. The task was to lead others to the summit from which they could behold the dawn of the new day.

News Reporters' Impressions

Significantly, before they left, two newsmen, who some days earlier had not relished the prospect of their latest assignment, spoke freely. Their weeks with these missionaries and younger church leaders, products of earlier missionary endeavor, had worked a great change. "The average person," said one, "imagines the missionary as a lone individual with a Bible under his arm somewhere out in a wilderness. And a lot of people think that giving for missions is like pouring money down a hole. The missionaries we've seen are not out just to convert individuals to add numbers to the churches. They have a whole program of social work, medicine, and education. To see that in foreign countries the enterprise is composed of real churches with real problems is news to us."

The other began, "If all your church members could sit through a conference such as this, you'd never need to worry again about their giving."

And to this the first quickly added, "I used to think that it didn't matter whether I contributed to missions or not. If I didn't, the next fellow would. But I don't have that feeling any longer. I have a completely new conception of missions — especially this business of their being a two-way affair!"

Whitby's Final Days

In the two days that remained after the remarkable agreement between the younger and older churches, the conference went on to determine priorities and to chart the next steps in the Christian world mission. To these another chapter is devoted. Delegates will remember the alert mind and the pointed suggestions of Dr. Ralph E. Diffendorfer, executive secretary of the Methodist Board of Missions in New York, and the contributions of his board secretary colleagues, Dr. Charles Leber of the Presbyterian Board of Foreign Missions and Dr. Jesse Wilson of the American Baptist Foreign Mission Society. Fellow workers from England were also heard: the Reverend H. P. Thompson of the Society for the Propagation of the Gospel, Canon Max Warren, chaplain of the conference and general secretary of the Church Missionary Society, and Dr. A. M. Chirgwin of the London Missionary Society. Each morning and evening delegates met in formal worship. In complete dependence on God, they sought a plan for carrying out the Great Commission. But it was never more apparent than in these final days that individual prayers were ascending to the heavenly Father from moment to moment in each session. The council was dedicated to knowing the will of God, and how that dedication lived.

In one of the final services a hymn of German origin was sung from the multilingual hymnbook used at Whitby. Fittingly, the hymn, "The Work Is Thine," had been suggested by a young Javanese minister of the Batak Church. Dr. John Mackay, who conducted the worship, crystallized in the word "frontier" that world from which the conference had been drawn and to which it looked — a frontier of flame where revolution is seen in grim splendor, but a frontier where Jesus Christ inhabits the wilderness and enables men devoted to his redemptive will to face that frontier with him. At the close of another one of these services there were prayers in many languages coming freely from the hearts of those there made one. A man may speak fluently in several languages; but when his heart is open to God, he can pray only in the freedom of his mother tongue. And the prayers that came from the depths of Christian hearts were in German, in Suto, in Spanish, in Tamil, and in Danish. No one could translate them all, but in that united company of the Spirit in which they were uttered, all were understood. In such fashion was one heart attuned to another that as each delegate came to the conclusion of his prayer, he was joined in his own "Amen" by a united "Amen." The living bond, the reality of the fellowhip in Christ, was never more real. This was a unity which no man could create and which no man can sunder.

Those who went out from that fellowship knew that the wounds of the world were festering above a revolution already begun. Yet they knew that the Great Commission of their Lord must be fulfilled in this world. The prospect was utterly staggering. But it produced no despairing futility. What it did generate was a tremendous, propulsive burst of sober, courageous hope. This hope was born of no calculated balancing of the possible with the impossible. It came from a depth of insight into that which cannot be shaken, into that which gives meaning to all of life and history — the love and power of God in Christ. Its authenticity was seen time and again in the lives of individual persons. Its glory was made real in the unity of fellowship experienced at Whitby. This hope was Whitby, for at Whitby tomorrow had been lived.

Chapter Four

INTERPRETING THE GOSPEL IN THE NEW DAY

W HAT HAS THE CHURCH TO SAY TO THE TOMORROW that is here? We have seen something of the revolutionary age that is on us, with its possibilities for unequaled tragedy and for unprecedented good. We have reminded ourselves that the church is in a better position than ever before to mold the entire human race. In only a few remote countries is it without representatives. Never before has this been true. Even during the past three and a half stormy decades the church has grown. Christianity is more deeply rooted among more peoples than it or any other religion or any set of ideas has ever been. Christians are being knit into a world-wide fellowship. This fact, as we have seen, was vividly demonstrated at Whitby. In the small company that gathered there the church of tomorrow was present, "from every nation, from all tribes and peoples and tongues," bound together in trust and love through a common faith and experience. The church of tomorrow is a minority in a world that does not understand it or its genius, that seems to be basically hostile to it and yet to be wistfully groping toward it — at times frantically — for the meaning of life that it preserves and for the kind of fellowship that it achieves. What is the message of the church to that world? How shall it be expressed to carry conviction?

In the yesterday that is passing the church made a contribution that is only beginning to be appreciated. Through the efforts of the minorities that were gripped by the Gospel, schools were planted across the frontiers of European settlements in the Americas, movements that led to the abolition of Negro slavery were begun, foundations for the profession of nursing were laid, and the dream was nurtured and the machinery sketched for the substitution of order for anarchy in the relations between nations. Through these minorities — and they were very small, for those who really believed in the world-wide mission of the church were few — the Gospel was proclaimed and Christian communities were planted and nourished in all the continents. Among people after people languages were reduced to writing, schools were begun, modern medicine and nursing were introduced, public health services were inaugurated, improved methods of agriculture were brought in, relief was given to sufferers from famine, means were devised for teaching the blind to read, and the Bible in whole or in part was translated into more than a thousand tongues and distributed by the millions of copies. All of this work in lands outside the Occident was accomplished by a missionary staff that, counting Roman Catholics and Protestants, was never above 60,000 at any time, and at an expense to the churches of the Occident that seldom reached $100,000,000 a year. If Protestants alone are taken into account, the totals were never above 30,000 missionaries and a cost of $70,000,000 a year. These totals were approached only in an unusual burst after World War I. In the reaction from that effort and after the great depression of 1929 the totals were much lower. That this meager force, distributed over three-fourths of the land surface of the globe, should have accomplished such results is astounding and can be accounted for only on the ground of the living power of the Gospel. Moreover, we must also remember that democracy, as that term was defined in the age that is passing, had as its basic conception the supreme worth and dignity of the individual and that this belief, the core of democracy, was derived from the Christian faith.

Because of the achievements of yesterday, in the tomorrow that is here the church is in a better position than ever before to give its witness to all mankind. It has a world-wide rootage and a growing fellowship. What has it to say to the new age? What has it to do in that age? How shall it so speak and act that its message shall be relevant to that age? Can it meet the needs that the men of that day believe to be crucial? These are fundamental questions that the church must face. To them Whitby gave much of its time.

The Eternal Gospel

There is an eternal Gospel. It is this with which the church is entrusted. It is this which forms the core of its message in all ages and to all men. It is through this that men enter on their true life.

Our earliest written record of this Gospel is in the New Testament. Thus it was to the New Testament that Whitby went, as Christians must always go, for an authoritative description. Yet, even there no single statement fully outlines the Gospel. That Gospel is too great to be compressed neatly into one formula. It refuses to be confined to confessions of faith or creeds, for although they may and do help, even when they are drawn from the New Testament, they are less than true to that collection of books, itself so varied, if they claim to be complete and final. The longer and more elaborate they are, the more likely are they to miss the mark. The New Testament is too wise to insist that only one of its descriptions exhausts the full meaning of the Gospel. Yet again and again the attempt must be made to go back to the New Testament, to discern its central message, and to phrase it in terms that are both true to the New Testament and intelligible to those who are really seeking to understand what it contains. This Whitby did. We must try to reproduce what was expressed there. In doing so we shall not quote exactly many phrases or merely summarize. We must endeavor to enter into the spirit of what was said and to capture it in fresh words.

First of all, we must always remember that the New Testament term is Gospel, "Good News." The word "Christianity" never occurs in the New Testament. Instead, the changes are rung on the Good News — news so amazing as at first to seem incredible, too good to be true. It was news that the disciples for joy could scarcely believe. This fact was true in New Testament times. It is true today.

The earliest summary of the content of that Good News or glad tidings was by Jesus himself. It was: " . . . the time is fulfilled, and the kingdom of God is at hand; repent and believe in the Gospel." It spoke of the reign or kingdom of God. This, obviously, is a society, a community in which God's will is done. In the prayer most familiar to Christians the reign of God is so described: "thy kingdom come, thy will be done on earth as it is in heaven." As Professor Baillie declared at Whitby: "The burden of our Lord's message was that a new age was about to dawn, and that men must make up their minds at once whether they were going to belong to it and share in the blessedness of its consummation, or continue to live as children of the old age and share in the doom which awaited it."

That kingdom is so utterly different from the world about it that to enter it, even to see it, requires what is best described as a new birth. "Unless one is born anew, he cannot see . . . he cannot enter the kingdom of God."

The new age was marked by the coming of that kingdom. That kingdom was present, but it had not yet fully come. It was both a present reality and a future hope. So, we may add, it is today. It is already here, foreshadowed and in part realized in the Christian community, but it has by no means fully arrived. We look for its consummation.

Central in that kingdom is love, love not as that word is often loosely employed, but in a special, quite different, and much grander sense. The Greek word in the New Testament is *agapē*. It is partially described in the thirteenth chapter of *First Corinthians*. It is the characteristic of God himself. "God is *agapē*." This love of God is closely connected with another word, "grace," which again and again recurs in the New Testament. "Grace" means the unmerited love of God. Men can never earn this love. They cannot deserve it. Yet it is of the very essence of God. "Herein is love, not that we loved God but that he loved us." Because God loves us we should love one another.

At the very heart of the Gospel is an act, or rather a series of events "which are all part of a grand event." Through this series of events God was doing something decisive, something that became the focus and turning point in human history. In these events God's love expressed itself. God spoke through the Word, which was God himself and which became flesh and dwelt among men. Jesus of Nazareth, Jesus Christ, the "anointed,"

God incarnate, in some strange and utterly unique way both man and God, was conceived of the Holy Spirit, born of Mary; he taught, healed, was crucified, died, and was buried, rose from the dead, and ever lives. All these events are part of a whole. If any one of them had not occurred, the act would have been incomplete. The cross is central. Here is the costly self-giving love of God, "who did not spare his own Son but gave him up for us all." "Christ died for our sins." He himself bore our sins in his body on the tree." "God shows his love for us in that while we were yet sinners Christ died for us." Yet the Cross takes its significance from the One who died on the Cross, from his nature, his birth, his life, his deeds, and his teachings, and the Cross would have spelled irretrievable defeat were it not for the resurrection. Moreover, even the resurrection did not complete the set of events. It was followed by the coming of the Holy Spirit. The Holy Spirit transformed the lives of those who "believed."

In this word "believe" is another aspect of the Gospel. The familiar New Testament verse that as nearly as any one single brief passage summarizes the Gospel is: "God so loved the world that he gave his only begotten son that whosoever believeth in him should not perish, but have everlasting life." Here is the self-giving love of God in Christ, with the promise of eternal life to those who "believe." "Believe," as the word is here used and as it is repeatedly employed through the New Testament, has more in it than intellectual assent. It includes that assent, but it means the commitment of the entire self. It means complete trust, the response of the entire personality. It is what the New Testament often calls "faith." It is man's glad, amazed, humble acceptance of God's love in Christ.

It is also part of the Gospel that through this response to God's love, through "belief" or "faith," men enter one by one the kingdom of God. This also means entering on eternal life. So radical is this change that it is described as being born again, raised from the dead, entering into life. It is accompanied by a fresh outlook. "Old things have passed away; and behold all things are become new." Those who have experienced it are "new creations." Their sins are forgiven and part of the forgiveness is the power to overcome sin, to be emancipated from the bondage of sin. The sin for which men need forgiveness and from which the Gospel frees them is not merely specific acts and habits, although it includes these. It is a basic twist of character, a fundamental self-centeredness, that makes satisfaction of the self's desires the main goal of longing and endeavor. The change may come spectacularly and abruptly. It may come by stages. Always, if it is real, it is followed by growth. Eternal life in the New Testament sense is not merely endless existence. That might be hell. Eternal life is fellowship with God; it is knowing God. Its chief characteristic is love, the kind of love that is seen in God in Christ. The goal of that life and of that growth is "being filled unto all the fullness of God," being perfect, as God is perfect.

Another phase of the Good News is the emergence of a fellowship of those who have entered upon this new life. It is a fellowship bound together by love, the love that God has shown in Christ. Its members are to be "tenderhearted, forgiving one another, even as God for Christ's sake hath forgiven" them. Its members know that they have "passed from death unto life" because they love the brethren. This fellowship, this society, is the church. It was not perfect in New Testament times — as the New Testament clearly shows. It is not perfect now. In its visible manifestations, it was divided then. It is divided now. Yet within it worked in New Testament days and is working now a power that makes for unity in love. Part of the marvel of Whitby was the degree to which that unity had grown and the foretaste it gave of the unity of the world-wide church.

We have already spoken of the Holy Spirit. The Holy Spirit is the living God at work in the world. It is through the Spirit that men are convicted of their sin, turn to God, and are born again. It is through the Spirit that the characteristic "fruits" of the Christian life appear — "love, joy, peace, long-suffering, gentleness, goodness, faith, meekness, self-control." It is on the working of God through the Holy Spirit that ultimately the hope of the world depends.

One other feature of the eternal Gospel must be mentioned. The Gospel centers around an act of God in history. Through it God continues to operate in the human scene. The Gospel is not confined to history. It began before history. "In the beginning was the Word, and the Word was with God, and the Word was God. . . . All things were made through him." The Gospel reaches beyond history. It speaks of eternal life. It declares the purpose of God to be to "gather together in one all things in Christ, both which are in heaven and which are on earth." The Gospel is both this-worldly and other-worldly. Herein lies much of its greatness. It deals with men in the midst of time but it knows that a man who has entered on eternal life cannot be bound by time, but goes on beyond time. Here men are living both in time and in eternity. The community of love of which the Gospel speaks and which it creates is here in time and is growing. In the tomorrow that is here it is demonstrating a love that rises above barriers of race, class, and nation, and is making for reconciliation and healing. It is not yet perfect, nor can it be within history. For its perfection and the perfection of those who are its members we must look beyond history to that eternity where time is no more. That its perfection will come we are assured. This is the hope that helps to give to man the high dignity that is one of the unique characteristics of the Gospel and makes for meaning in the otherwise frustrating drama of human history. Hope is an aspect of the Gospel that we must always remember as we seek to understand it, interpret it, and formulate what we can rightly expect of it within history.

Interpreting the Gospel to the Tomorrow That Is Here

How shall the eternal Gospel be interpreted to the men of the tomorrow that is here? How shall it be so expressed that its relevance will be apparent and that it can perform its rightful mission? The Gospel remains the same, but in each new age it must be put into terms that are pertinent to the distinctive needs of that age. One of the preparatory papers for Whitby bore the striking title: "Waiting for the Word." In it was expressed the haunting urgent longing of our age for an authentic Word from God. That Word is already here. "The Word is near you, on your lips and in your heart (that is, the Word of faith which we preach)." Yet, as always, that Word must be expressed in convincing fashion.

In one sense the needs of men do not change. They are the same from age to age. Man is ever searching for the answer to the mysteries of life and death, for the meaning of life, for the release from his enslavement to sin, and for God, even when he is not aware of the precise cause of his restlessness and does not know the name of God. In every age the eternal Gospel speaks to him. Often the Bible, unaided, is the effective messenger. In the next chapter is a striking instance of this. More frequently the Gospel is unmistakably and convincingly conveyed through a loving heart that is a living demonstration of the nature and power of the Gospel. In the next chapter a number of contemporary examples of this type of demonstration evidenced at Whitby in men and women from different cultural and national backgrounds will also be given. In every age, the Bible and transformed, loving lives are the best agents of the Gospel. Men are not to be won by any fabric of words, no matter how intelligently framed or how seemingly suited to the vocabulary and special needs of the age. They are won by the contagion of life upon life. One loving soul sets another on fire.

Yet each age also has needs peculiar to itself and has its own vocabulary. In seeking to meet these needs and to use this vocabulary, Christians are in peril of twisting the meaning of the Gospel and thereby corrupting it. This danger is always present and can seldom if ever be fully overcome. Yet it is a risk that must be taken. The church partially succumbed to it when it won the Roman Empire. Out of its triumph came the Roman Catholic Church — what some one has called "the ghost of the Roman Empire." Protestantism owed its appeal partly to its response to the demands of its day — rising nationalism and the yearning for personal dignity, opportunity, and freedom. But in consequence it became gravely distorted by them and has both contributed to and been infected by exaggerated nationalism, rampant individualism, and exclusively this-worldly concerns. Christians of the tomorrow that is here must not permit this danger to deter them. We must seek to speak to the special demands of our age, but in such fashion that the Gospel in practice shall be as little compromised as possible.

First of all, then, if the church is to fulfill its mission in the tomorrow that is here, it must proclaim, as always at its best it has proclaimed, the eternal Gospel as the answer to the continuing, persistent, unchanging needs of men. It must seek to do this to all men, everywhere. It must endeavor to make disciples of all nations. To be true to the commission of its Lord the church can never be content to aim at less.

In the second place, the church must not be too eager to make the Gospel acceptable. The Gospel was not intelligible to those who first heard it. To the Greeks it seemed to be foolishness and to the Jews a stumbling block. It will always seem strange; it can never be fully assimilated to any culture without losing its savor.

In the third place, in an age of revolution the church must demonstrate that it is not a bulwark of an outmoded privileged order but that the Gospel is revolutionary, and in a more thoroughgoing and constructive sense than is any competitor. The Gospel proclaims a newer order than does any of its rivals. This order puts secondary what most of its new competitors make primary — food, clothing, and shelter — and yet it declares that if men only place first the reign of God all these material benefits will come. This, it may be added, is literal fact. The material things of this life will be far more assured if men live by the ideals of the kingdom of God than if they follow other faiths. These rival faiths, whether capitalism, communism, or totalitarian nationalism in any of its forms, breed hate and strife that destroy the very possessions they are supposed to secure. The Gospel places a far higher value on the individual than do any of its rivals, whether old or new. Though at times interpreted imperfectly by churches, it has accomplished more for the dignity of man than has any other force that the world has known. If really put into practice and released in all its power, it would do even more.

In the fourth place, in a world where physical distress and suffering are more widespread than ever and cruelty, deliberate or callous, has mounted, the church must give relief both to body and spirit by sacrificial, unostentatious, compassionate self-giving. It must also pioneer in devising and demonstrating methods for the removal of at least some of the bases of that suffering — in rural reconstruction, in the right kind of education, and in the lightening of tensions among groups, races, and nations.

In the fifth place, in a world that is desperately longing for security and for the peace between nations that is so essential to security, the Gospel at first sight seems disappointing. It declares that those who purpose to be disciples of Christ must renounce all they have and take up their cross and follow him. It also states Christ's warning that he came not to bring peace but a sword. We must not blink the fact that it contains these warnings. Yet no other single factor has made more powerfully for peace among the nations. Today the world-wide church is the most widespread, comprehensive fellowship known to man. It has grown in spite of the tragic wars of the present century. More than ever must it clearly demonstrate in its own life the unity and peace that the world craves. It has made a beginning, but only a beginning. The fellowship at Whitby that embraced a wide variety of races and nations must be expanded until it is experienced by all who name the name of Christ. The church must face the world, as Dr. Van Dusen declared at Whitby, with a united strategy, a united message, a united program, a united leadership, and a united community — a united community made possible by radical conversion, by commanding rededication in the presence of one Christ and one world.

The Impossible but Assured Goal

Christians must not be deterred by the magnitude of the task. In a day when the opposing forces are massive and aggressive and appear to be dominant, and when Christians constitute minorities — in most lands small minorities — the temptation is strong to be content with defense and with holding what has been achieved. That way lie both treason and defeat. The New Testament picture of the church is one of besieging, not being besieged. It is evil that is on the defensive. The church is attacking. "The gates of hell," the promise reads, "shall not prevail against it." If Christians pray sincerely "thy kingdom come, thy will be done on earth as it is in heaven," they must do whatever lies in them to answer that prayer. They have the commission laid upon them to "make disciples of all nations, baptizing them . . . teaching them to observe all things" that Jesus commanded the little intimate circle of his immediate followers. This commission, it need scarcely be said, is breath-taking — to teach all men to live up to the ideals of the Sermon on the Mount. These ideals are so demanding as seemingly to be beyond the attainment of the choicest few. Yet, if Christians are true to their faith they can never be content with anything less than this goal. The church must embark on a program of world-wide evangelism, and that evangelism must have as an ideal the full sweep of the Lord's prayer and of the Great Commission.

If the church is to live up to its mission in this tomorrow that is upon us, there must be revival and thoroughgoing reform. The church as we now know it can never accomplish the task. It is too divided, it has too much "conformed to this world," the bulk of its members have too generally accepted in practice the standards of the community really to carry through the Great Commission. What is needed is a reform even more drastic than that of the Protestant Reformation. The church must so give itself to its Lord that it will discover the power of the Gospel as never before, or, rather, be discovered by it.

What hope can there be that these goals will be attained? Is it not sheer lack of realism to dream that the church will be so stirred, so revitalized and reformed, that it will become a sufficiently living force to attain its goal? Even if it were to be thus revived, is not the goal so high and the world so corrupt that the Great Commission is a fantastic impossibility? Again and again and in many different ways the New Testament seems to warn us that we cannot expect God's will to be done fully within history. There is to be a consummation, a "harvest," and the wheat and the weeds are both to grow until that decisive event.

These questions, so sobering because they seem to be so in accord with experience and with the New Testament, must be faced, but they need neither dishearten nor deter us. The ideal and the command are there. They are obviously of God. In our heart of hearts we know that they are inherent in the very nature of our faith. So far as lies in us we must be true to God. The power and the fruitage, like the command, are not ours but God's. Again and again experience has proved that as men venture out on the commands and promises of God a power flows into them that is not of themselves and that transforms them.

Results follow, out of all proportion to the human effort expended and often quite unexpected. Who would have anticipated the present world-wide Christian fellowship at the beginning of the recent era of Protestant missions? Who would have predicted all the revolutions and the healing, constructive movements the world over that have followed the efforts of the lone individuals and small groups that have staffed and supported the missionary enterprise? The church itself had its beginning in a little company, approximately the size of that at Whitby, followers of a crucified and, from the point of view of the casual observer, frustrated and defeated leader. We dare not wait for the reformation of the entire church. Great revivals and reforms have always started with individuals who became the attractive centers of small groups. We who write these words and those who read them must begin now. We must give ourselves afresh to God as disciples of his Son and trust his Holy Spirit to use us as he will. "Be steadfast, immovable, always abounding in the work of the Lord, knowing that in the Lord your labor is not in vain."

Chapter Five

THE ETERNAL GOSPEL REALIZED
IN LIFE

WHITBY PROVIDED A REMARKABLE DEMONSTRATION of the transforming power of the eternal Gospel in human life. Nearly one in ten of its members was a "first-generation Christian" — one who had not inherited his Christian allegiance, but had himself come directly into Christianity from a nominal or a non-Christian background. Consider the significance of that fact. One tenth of those at Whitby entrusted with future plans for the Christian world mission had entered the community of Christian faith within their adult lifetimes. The wonder, glory, and power of the Gospel are often most strikingly seen in such lives, transformed and made strong.

One of Whitby's most memorable experiences came in a session not originally scheduled, when several first-generation Christians shared with those present the stories of their conversions. These delegates, whose homelands encircle the globe, offered living proof that the needs of men are universal and that the appeal of the Gospel is limited by neither race nor culture. While all were born in a day that is passing, all are still in early middle life and are leaders in the tomorrow that is here.

The backgrounds from which these people came into the Christian faith varied. One was reared in a Chinese Confucian family. Still another had been an Indian Brahman. Two had been nominal Christians. One had come from a background of secularism in Europe. Finally, one who was present at that session and whose story is here recorded, although he did not speak, had been a Moslem Sufi in India. Each account is evidence that in the present tomorrow as in all the yesterdays, the Gospel speaks in every language to man's condition and that through it the miracle of the new birth is ever repeated.

A Chinese

Chen Wen-yuen, the son of a Confucian scholar, was reared in the traditional Confucian pattern. In his family, as in many Chinese families, grandparents, parents, uncles, aunts, cousins, and children — thirty members — all lived under one roof, with the old grandmother as head of the family. When young Chen was thirteen, his parents sent him off to school, to the Anglo-Chinese College of Foochow, a Methodist institution. This was the lad's first contact with the foreigner, with the Bible, and with the church. "All these were often hostile to my thinking," he narrated, "and I joined a student group opposed to the Christian religion and shortly became its ringleader."

Chen's school days came before the establishment of the Republic of China when students wore the then common Chinese queue — the long hair braid. In class, however, there was one student who wore his hair short. "I was much attracted to him," said Chen. "He was president of the student Y.M.C.A. and leader of the Student Volunteer Group. As we became better friends, he offered to share his room with me." Much as Chen wanted to accept this offer of friendship, he was dubious, because this student was a Christian. Although he was much impressed with this particular Christian, he wanted no part of Christianity. Yet the student as a friend and leader appealed to Chen so much that he decided to try living with him on one condition. "We became roommates with the understanding that he would not talk to me about the Christian faith. This agreement he faithfully kept."

Each Sunday afternoon the Christian student went out with one of the missionaries to preach on street corners. One, two — six months passed and in all that time Chen's roommate never mentioned Christianity to him. But Chen's curiosity was aroused. What did these Christians preach about? One afternoon he accompanied his friend to observe the street meeting and find out. What the Christian student said burned deeply in Chen's heart, but while he spoke, an older Chinese in the crowd began to taunt him. "Look at that young Christian without a queue! Only the foreigners wear short hair. Anyone who becomes a Christian becomes a foreigner!"

Although he was not a Christian, Chen had learned deeply to admire and respect his roommate. This unwarranted attack on him was too much. Boldly proclaiming what was fact, Chen came to the defense of his friend. "What this man says is not so. *The queue is foreign!* It was forced on the Chinese by the Manchus three hundred years ago!" and then, inspired by his own force, he went on, not knowing why he said what he did next. "If Christianity is true, it is not foreign. Any religion which is true *is true anywhere*. It cannot be foreign."

That night Chen could not sleep. He was miserable. The months of close day-to-day living with his Christian roommate had had a pronounced effect on him. Thoughts of the afternoon flooded his mind, and he realized that he was living without Christ. The first rays of the morning sun pouring into his room illuminated the picture that hung above his roommate's bed, a picture of Christ praying in Gethsemane. Chen's heart was stirred. "I saw that Christ was praying for sinners. He was praying for me. I went over and knelt by my friend's bed before that picture, and something then and there happened to me. I told my friend that my battle was over. I would receive Christ into my heart. When I went outside, the whole universe seemed wonderfully different, more beautiful. Even the words of Confucius, Mencius, and the other sages seemed more vivid than before. It was a new world, and I was a new creature in it."

After that it was not always easy. "But I realized," said Chen, "that the Word of God is dynamic. It did not stop with me as did the words of Confucius and Mencius. I became restless to declare it to my own family. The Word of God in me had to grow, to burst out in an explosion — and the first object of that explosion was my grandmother. She consented to go to church only because it was her grandson who asked her. But the explosion was successful! When my grandmother became a Christian, she was sixty-four. Then she, the oldest member of the family, and I, the youngest, began to win the others. She worked from the top down and I from the bottom up. And today the great majority of my family are Christians."

When he had completed this part of his story, Bishop Chen attached a postscript, "There are four points I would like to add which I draw from my own experience. First, God has various ways of communicating his Word. Second, a little incident in life may serve as a channel through which God speaks to a man. Third, God's Word fulfills the sayings of the Chinese sages; it enriches, completes, and brings them back to life. Fourth, God's Word has an explosive power. It also grows and overflows one's life." [1]

A Cuban

When Francisco Garcia was born, his parents were members of the Roman Catholic Church in Cuba, and he was baptized in that church. As he grew up, he attended church regularly. However, after his twelfth birthday he lost interest and, as did so many of his friends, regarded churchgoing to be for women and children. At Whitby Señor Garcia declared, "From the time I was twelve until I was twenty, I had no real Christian life. When I was converted, I was not an active Roman Catholic communicant. I said my prayers every night and considered myself a Catholic, but I had never seen a Bible and had never heard a real sermon. I had an idea of many saints and of a God remote from me, but I had no interest in the church."

One day a friend asked the young señor to visit a meeting of Christians in his home. The youthful Garcia was not interested and turned down the invitation, but when it was repeated for three weeks in succession, he relented. In that small home meeting for the first time he heard a Cuban minister preach. He returned again and again. The Gospel proclaimed there awakened his deepest interest. His next decision was to attend the near-by Presbyterian church regularly. When the church gave him a New Testament, he read it eagerly.

Francisco Garcia continued to go to the church and to read

[1] The Reverend Bishop Chen Wen-yuen received his B.A. and M.A. from Syracuse University and his Ph.D. from Duke University. One-time acting president of Fukien Christian University, he is now honorary general secretary of the National Christian Council of China and a bishop of the Methodist Church.

his New Testament. And then, just before Holy Week, he attended a series of special services, at which time, he explained, "An invitation was given to all who wanted to accept Christ as a personal Saviour. When the invitation came, I stood and confessed my Lord. I did this because I knew that I was a sinner and needed a Saviour. Following that decision, I attended for three months a training class for church membership. At the conclusion of the course, I was admitted into the church."

"Since then," continued Garcia, "I have had my ups and downs in the Christian faith. But I saw all along the glory in the lives of Christians who are wholly consecrated to the Lord, and that helped me to give my life completely. Later the Spirit of God led me to dedicate my life to his service. And for fifteen years I have been preaching the same Gospel and Lord who saved me. I know only one way that I can save people from sin, and that is to tell them forthrightly what sin is in their own lives and how Jesus Christ is the Saviour of all mankind." [1]

An Indian

"I belong to a group of people so near to the kingdom of God that it is difficult for any member to enter that kingdom. They have become so deeply entrenched in themselves and are so proud of their history that they are the bitterest opponents of the Christian faith and church." The Reverend Paul Rama-seshan was speaking of India's highest caste, the Brahmans, among whom he had been reared and educated. One's thoughts immediately traveled back to Paul and the Pharisees. But he

[1] Educated at Toccoa Falls Bible Institute and the Evangelical Seminary of Puerto Rico, the Reverend Francisco de la Paz Garcia y Serpa is pastor of the First Presbyterian Church in Havana, Cuba.

went on, "So carefully were we segregated that not even normal contacts with Christians were possible."

One day something little short of an earthquake happened to young Ramaseshan that changed the entire course of his life. It was not a reasoned argument. It was a deep experience. But let him relate it. "An Indian Christian came to our village regularly to preach, and just as regularly over a period of six months a gang of boys, of whom I was the leader, made it their sport to stone him and his party. One night after we had thrown our stones, I failed to run soon enough or fast enough and was caught by one of the preaching party. I looked into the eyes of the man who held me. The affectionate sympathy and the abounding love that I saw in his face completely changed my sense of values. This man, instead of cuffing me, treated me kindly and spoke to me lovingly. Then and there I promised to read whatever he would give me."

Ramaseshan, the stone thrower, received that day a copy of the four Gospels. Recalling the experience, he continued, "Something that I could not understand gripped me in the words of the Gospels. Although I could not comprehend all their meaning, I read them always with this man's loving face before me. There was something in the book that gave me a passion. Then in the providence of God I was led on to someone who could help me. He became my 'father in Christ.' In his fellowship I found the meaning of love — the love that had shone in the face of that first Christian who spoke to me." A Brahman had been found of God, and he accepted Jesus Christ as his Lord and Saviour.

The decision to become a Christian was costly. It meant the loss of old friends. It meant severing all family ties. The legal career for which his family had been grooming him had to be forgotten. When the Brahman Ramaseshan became a Christian, he was certain in mind and heart that God wanted him to enter the ministry. That meant turning his back on everyone and everything in life dear to him. Yet it was as nothing, for as he says, "In return I have found Christ as Lord." [1]

A Filipina

The reader is already acquainted with Dr. Josefa Ilano. Her father and other relatives had rebelled against the Roman Catholic Church in the Philippines. However, when she was a young girl, she was sent to her grandmother, a devout Catholic, and reared by her in that faith. When Josefa reached college age, she attended Silliman University, a Presbyterian school. But the college girl was not happy. Religiously she was hungry — seeking; for, as she said, "My life was completely empty. I had prayed to the Virgin Mary and to all the women saints — never to the men. But I had no Saviour."

During her course at Silliman, Miss Ilano attended one of a series of evangelistic meetings that were then being held. Of them she said, "I went for six nights, but was not especially interested. However, on the seventh night, I heard the words, 'I am the resurrection and the life.' 'I am the light of the world.' And then it was as though I saw Christ's hands stretched out and heard his voice saying, 'Come unto me all ye that labor and are heavy laden, and I will give you rest.' Suddenly I felt tired and weary, searching and groping in the darkness for the light. My life had been sheltered, and I had been provided with every

[1] The Reverend Paul Ramaseshan is a minister of the Methodist Church and principal of the South India Training Institution, Madras, India.

material thing. Yet something was lacking. Life was empty because I did not have a personal Saviour. This I knew on that seventh night of the meetings, and so I accepted Christ and found my Saviour and Lord."

When Josefa Ilano was graduated from college, she went on to the University of the Philippines for her medical training. It is never easy for a woman in medical school where virtually all the faculty members and students are men. But there was another far more serious difficulty. Miss Ilano, explaining it, said, "I was persecuted. Difficulties and obstacles were put in my way because I had accepted the Evangelical faith. Conflicting thoughts began to crowd my mind, and so I began writing to the minister who had baptized me. When he answered, he mentioned only Bible verses. This led me to read, to search, and to study the Bible. In this way I felt something growing within me, and with each passing year of my life, I knew that I was experiencing a slow, yet steadfast and ever-increasing spiritual growth because of him who was my Lord and Master, my guide and friend and personal Saviour."

To those who know Miss Ilano, it is evident that this growth continues in a remarkable fashion. She was flown to the United States for a speaking tour in 1946–1947 with two other Christian women from China and Japan. On the first day, at the dinner table, seated next to Mrs. Tamaki Uemura, the only woman allowed to leave Japan in two years after the war, she could not bring herself to speak to her Japanese colleague. She avoided her glance. Josefa Ilano's mind was filled with scenes of horror, pillage, and death caused by Japanese in the Philippines. She felt within that she could never forgive *any* Japanese for what she had seen and experienced.

That first night they were lodged in a women's college dormitory. The next morning Miss Ilano heard a knock at her door. When she opened it, there stood her Japanese companion. "Her head was bowed, and she asked only, 'May we go to breakfast together?' We walked in silence through the long corridor, went downstairs, and there entered a small room alone. When Mrs. Uemura looked at me, her face was filled with humility and radiant love such as I had never seen before, and she said, 'Dr. Ilano, will you forgive me and my people for the suffering inflicted on you in the Philippines?' In that moment we both fell to our knees and prayed only as can Christians who have suffered much. Together in humble confession of our sins before God, we knew that the love of Christ was filling our hearts and drawing us together. After that we cried, but we went in to breakfast together, smiling. The people could see what had happened, and they were very happy. On that trip Mrs. Uemura and I became fast friends. It was she in her humble, saintly life who taught me the real meaning of Christ's love. Through her I learned forgiveness and that there is nothing that can separate those who are united by the love of Christ." [1]

A Belgian

"From shirt sleeves to shirt sleeves in three generations" is the familiar story of a family's economic rise and fall. It has its religious counterpart. Colonel Robert Ernest van Goethem comes of an old Belgian bourgeois family that can trace its ancestry back for centuries. His great-grandfather had been

[1] Miss Josefa M. Ilano received her B.A. from Silliman University and her M.D. from the University of the Philippines in 1927. A member of the United Evangelical Church, she is an elder in her local church in Manila. A practising physician, she is also a recognized leader in the Philippine Federation of the Evangelical Churches.

converted by a colporteur of the British and Foreign Bible Society. His grandfather, more interested in philosophy and business, was a nominal Christian and left his father's church for a more formal congregation. His parents were "free thinkers." The cycle from non-Christian to non-Christian took only three generations. Van Goethem himself, reared a secularist, is now chief of Protestant chaplains of the Belgian Forces.

When young Robert was growing up, he never heard any discussion of religion in his home. He was educated at a school in which no religion was taught and where he and all his friends, on political grounds, were anti-Roman Catholic. In 1916, with a group of students on their way to Holland to join the army, he was taken prisoner by the Germans. His one consuming desire in prison was to be free — to be able to do as he desired. With his release in 1918 young van Goethem indulged himself in wild and reckless living. His father, somewhat disturbed by his mode of life, decided that what he needed to settle him was a stint as a gentleman farmer. He bought his son a 160-acre farm in Alberta and shipped him off to Canada.

Van Goethem's habits were not readily changed. "Besides," as he said, "the farm was 160 acres of bush and called only for hard work. I spent most of my time in the town, and in a short while, through gambling, lost all that I had, including the farm. At the time I was conscious of the fact that I was doing wrong. I thought a change of environment would change me, and so I went to Alaska to find a new beginning. It was the same thing there for a year and a half. I was still restless. Then I went down the coast as far as Hollywood and Los Angeles. All the time I was vainly searching for something that would satisfy me."

The discontented Belgian, seeking new sights and new experiences, was wandering around the streets of Los Angeles one Thanksgiving evening when he passed a group of young Christians. They were conducting a Gospel meeting out on the street, and one of them invited the stranger to come into the church. As van Goethem explained, "I had never been in a church, so I went in and listened to the preaching of the Gospel. I could not really understand what was said, because all the terms they used were like a foreign language to me. But I began to think. For a long time I had been searching. It had never occurred to me to look in a church for what I was seeking. And there in that church the spirit of God convicted me of sin. What I had been trying to escape came to me. At the close of the meeting the good man in charge said that if anyone present wished to be saved from sin, he should believe in Jesus Christ as his Saviour. I did not know much about it then, but in those words God and the whole of heaven seemed to open to me. I said 'Yes,' for those words were a light to my soul."

When the service was concluded, the minister met with him and asked him if he did not wish to pray. To this the young convert frankly replied, "I do not know how." As he continued the story, "The minister then taught me the prayer of the publican, 'Lord, be merciful to me a sinner.' This became my prayer, and I went home, knowing that something had changed me. . . . Night after night I went to those meetings, and the young people continued to help me read and understand the New Testament. Day after day we prayed. With things now changed in my life, I wanted only to go back to Belgium, and I decided to return to my home. No longer was I seeking a change of environment, for I had experienced a change of heart. God's Word was life to me."

During World War II van Goethem was again in prison — but this time for his preaching. "It was different now," he said. "Even though I was in solitary confinement, I had my Bible. God was with me and I never felt so free. Secretly, I managed to communicate with the paratrooper next to me who was condemned to death. All he could say was, 'It is hell to be alone with oneself.' I replied, 'It is wonderful to be alone with God.' Then I managed to pass him my Bible, and we prayed together — always in secret. He read the Bible and was won to Christ. You may know the peace and joy which filled my heart when I learned that as he was put to death his last words were, 'It is wonderful to be alone with God.' " [1]

An Indian

Abdus-Subhan came from a long line of Indian sufis, the holy men of Islam who work magic and can repeat the Koran by heart. Reared as he was in the lore of Islam, Abdus — later called John — very early became a mystic. Before he was ten he had read the entire Koran and had begun to memorize it. He observed all the prayers and fasts, and with a holy passion he hated Christians. As a young boy he began his search for God. He became something of a worker of magic and was besieged by those who sought the benefits of his powers. And then, what heretofore had been unheard of, he became a sufi at the age of thirteen and was initiated into the secrets of that religious order. It became his purpose as a mystic to seek perfection and a true knowledge of God, and eventually to know union with Allah.

[1] Colonel Robert E. van Goethem was educated at the University of Brussels and later at the Bible Institute of Los Angeles and the Methodist Pastoral School of Belgium. A Methodist minister, he was recently made chief Protestant chaplain of the Belgian and Colonial Forces.

6578

One day a Moslem friend who had received a copy of a Gospel from an itinerant evangelist gave it to Abdus-Subhan. Abdus-Subhan ripped it apart, for his teacher had warned him that it contained words of blasphemy that would pollute the soul of a believer. But when later he received a second copy of one of the Gospels, an inner urge led him to read it. The result was startling. Abdus-Subhan saw nothing blasphemous in the Gospel, and its ethical standards were exalted. If Christians had invented the story, they would never have included the shameful death of the Master, or caused him to reappear only to his disciples while his enemies remained triumphant over his death. As the youthful sufi read, he became convinced that this was God's Word and Revelation! He had never seen or heard a missionary. He had read only one Gospel, but he said, "It was sufficient! I decided to become a Christian." God had found *him*.

The young lad could discover no one who would instruct him and make him a Christian, and so, securing a Bible, he went through it unaided and came to a fair understanding of Christianity. One day he saw a circular of the Young Men's Christian Association and paid that institution a visit. There he met a blind secretary who became his friend and taught him to pray. He found that "Prayer is not a bargain with God. It is a fellowship of a son with a father." The young man's heart flamed with the love of Christ. "Nothing would satisfy me but to become his follower by openly confessing him and professing his religion." When he did so in the Moslem school he was attending, he was cursed, spat upon, and expelled. At the same time he was refused Christian baptism and church membership because of his age!

The youth, whose life was given to Christ, some time later

gained admittance to an Anglican high school, and he became one of the most earnest Christians among the students. He preached on street corners. He visited hospitals, telling each patient about Christ. He was a zealous evangelist — still unbaptized. But when he reached his fifteenth year, he was baptized and shortly afterwards was confirmed in the Church of England.

John Subhan was still a mystic. His passion for personal evangelism waned, and his desire for lonely communion with Christ became more pronounced, finally leading him toward Rome. Nine years after his baptism he became a member of the Roman Catholic Church and began preparing for the priesthood. But after four years, convinced that the long hours he spent in mystic communion were not helping others to know God, and certain that some of the attitudes and teachings of his superiors were contradictory to his experience and understanding of the Bible, he left the Roman Catholic Church and returned to his Protestant faith.

Later as a teacher in a Methodist theological seminary, John Subhan was attracted by the people of that denomination because of their emphasis on personal experience and evangelism. He joined this church and soon became one of its ministers. He continued to be both teacher and minister and also became a recognized leader of the Christian church in India.

Speaking of the Christian life, John Subhan said, "No amount of reading about mountains can give that feeling of joy which a mountaineer experiences in actually climbing the steep peaks and living surrounded by mountain scenery. The Christian attitudes of life cannot be acquired by mere reading about them, but by living in personal contact with persons who embody them in their own lives. God is infinite and so there is no limit to his love, goodness, and purity. Thus it is that the more we live with him, the more we know of the divine qualities as he reveals them." [1]

The eternal Gospel is realized always in individual lives — transformed, made new, and imbued with a power that no human being can command. Still no one individual within himself and no one group of individuals within themselves can begin to know or achieve the fullness of life that is in Christ. After the Gospel had laid hold of him, how eagerly John Subhan looked for a fuller experience of the Christian life *in fellowship with other lives*. It was Mrs. Uemura whose loving spirit brought even new depth and understanding into Josefa Ilano's life, made new as it had been a quarter of a century earlier. Each person grows in the Christian life as he learns to receive the particular witness and contribution of other Christians. That is why every Christian needs the fellowship of the congregation and why every congregation needs the larger fellowship of the world Christian community.

Nor can an individual made new by the Gospel of Christ contain the gift of the new life within. That new life must express itself. It must be shared with others. Each testimony bears evidence to the fact. Such a life — a new creation — is never a life unto itself. Shot through with the glory and fire of God's loving gift, that life must ever be self-giving, for self-giving is

[1] The Reverend Bishop John A. Subhan received his B.A. from Allahabad and his B.D. from Serampore. He served at one time as lecturer at Bareilly Theological Seminary and then at the Henry Martyn School. Later he became pastor of the Central Methodist Church in Delhi. In 1944 he was made a bishop in the Methodist Church.

This account is based on "The Search of a Sufi," by Elmer T. Clark.

the essence of that by which it has been possessed and transformed.

The initial experience of the new life that is in Christ may come in a variety of ways: through the spoken word, through the written word, or through an experience that articulates without words the meaning of the Gospel. Yet it is always the shared experience of other saintly lives that brings this new life to its highest expression. It is the contagion of lives of Christlike love that makes Christians. It is always thus from one life to another that the Gospel has been made known. The communication of the Gospel depends not on thoughtful phraseology, but on living agents, because life alone can beget life.

Chapter Six

PARTNERS IN OBEDIENCE

THE TASK THAT CONFRONTS THE CHURCHES OF THE WORLD is one. The commission to that task is one, spoken *to all* who name the name of Christ. The challenge must be met unitedly.

That a united approach to the common task must be — can be — achieved by the younger and older churches of the world was made abundantly clear at Whitby. An equality, a mutuality, a shared partnership between the younger and older churches such as had never before been known was manifest there. There was no need to argue the necessity for more understanding between the two. What had once been discussed and hoped for was now a reality. In the very nature of things there are and will be differences between the younger and older churches. That fact is inescapable. But whereas in the past the relationship has been as that between parent and child, with the frequent recurrence of unhappy paternalism and undue dependence, now in truth the relationship is one between brothers who recognize that in their common sonship each has responsibilities for the other, and that, together, they have responsibilities for the world. This new partnership in obedience to God's will is part of the tomorrow that Whitby experienced as already here.

It was not always so. Western churches, the so-called "sending churches," provided the missionaries, supplied the money, and

supervised its expenditure. Unfortunately, too, some missionaries were imbued with an attitude of "the white man's burden."
Paternalism and the patriarchal missionary at the head of a
small Christian community were the all too common results.
These, of course, made difficult the widespread development of
first-rate indigenous leadership — nationals who could assume
full responsibility for the welfare of the church in their homeland.

On the other hand, there frequently has been among the
younger churches a too easy, complacent acceptance of continued dependency. Even today not more than 15 per cent of
the local congregations of the younger churches are totally
self-supporting. Some of the reasons for this must be considered
later. It has been most difficult, also, to claim the ablest men of
the younger churches for leadership in the church. This issues
from glaringly evident causes that must be met realistically
before any serious advance can be made. "Colonial churches"
have often resulted, with the difficulties that attend any colonial
relationship. When in the past representatives of the younger
and older churches met together in conference, the lines were
clearly drawn between them. Both shared responsibility for the
resultant friction, but each tended to recognize the other's
shortcomings only. Naturally, in conference this produced
heated discussions. The contrasting unanimity that marked
Whitby has already been noted.

Today the "colonial churches" are coming of age. Indeed,
some of the so-called "younger" churches in India are actually
older than one of the major denominations in the United States,
the Disciples of Christ. In fact, the distinction between the
terms "older" and "younger" became largely obsolete at

Whitby, proof of the coming of age of the younger churches. After a few minutes of wrestling with the problem of a fresh nomenclature, it was decided to retain the familiar terms for convenience only.

The effects of the war, with accompanying shifts in the financial status of the churches, the shared burdens, and the suffering together of missionaries with younger churchmen; the growing fellowship of the churches in the Ecumenical Movement; and the changing world scene in which communism, secularism, religious imperialism, mechanization, and depersonalization of life confront older and younger churches equally — at Whitby all these elements combined to create a new unity and urgency. In this changed relationship the whole problem of effecting mutuality disappeared. Instead, younger and older *together in an accomplished mutuality* undertook to outline a single program for doing *no less than carrying the Gospel to the whole world*. This was the difference between Madras and Whitby.

Evangelism, the evangelization of the whole world — expectant evangelism — in the face of an unprecedented massing of forces opposed to Christianity — this is the one, immediate, supreme challenge confronting the church today. This is not the special task of the younger churches, nor of the older churches, but of *both*. World evangelism — the evangelization of every area of life by men and women ablaze with the fire of God, torches flaming with the Gospel of Christ — is the task of the church. The compelling urgency of a world whose agony now may drive it to one blinding flash of atomic death leaves the church no time for considered alternatives. The church has but one choice, like it or not, meet it or not. The very desperation of the world — worse now than during the war — gives the church its one unexampled opportunity. It is momentary. But in God's grace the moment has been thrust before the church. The task — urgent, of unimaginable magnitude, thrilling beyond the comprehension of man's mind — is the fulfillment of the Great Commission.

Confronting an unprecedented world challenge, Whitby categorically declared that all churches together must revive and deepen their own life that the spiritual nurture of the individual Christian may be strengthened. If the church is to be the church, it will be so to the extent that it produces within and without a far-reaching revival. With equal emphasis Whitby asserted the necessity that every local church inculcate within each member a sense of responsibility as a member of the holy catholic church — the church universal. The unsurpassed glory of realized kinship in the ecumenical community of world Christianity is the divine intention for all who confess Jesus Christ as Lord. It was never meant to be the exclusive privilege of the leaders of the churches. But the *sine qua non* for the whole of the larger accomplishment is the training by the churches of *every member according to his ability for the work of Christian witness*. Wherever that is accomplished, each layman will be bearing his own testimony in seeking the sanctification of the life of the home, in winning the younger generation for Christ, and in permeating all common life with Christian principles and ideals. When that witnessing is effective, it will instill in every Christian as a son of God a sense of total stewardship for the maintenance of the existing church and for the great evangelistic task ahead.

On younger and older churches alike the demand of the hour

is to establish pioneer work in all areas of the world where the Gospel has not yet been preached and where the church has not yet taken root. But within this partnership, in obedience to the Divine Commission, one special charge is given to the older churches and one to the younger churches. To the older churches the commission is to make compelling to youth the needs of younger churches and to enlist young people in the world mission in numbers far greater than ever before. It must be admitted with shame that among the older churches there are many that have not yet taken seriously the obligation of the Great Commission and that accept grudgingly, if at all, the duty to make their ablest men and women available for the work of the younger churches. There are still instances of church leaders who discourage rather than encourage recruitment among those best suited for missionary service. This must be set aright. For the younger churches there is the call to put away once for all every thwarting sense of dependence on the older churches, and on the true ground of absolute spiritual equality and under the guidance of the Holy Spirit, "to bear their own distinctive witness in the world, as the instrument by which God wills to bring to Christ the whole population of the lands in which they dwell."

Partners in Finance

It takes money to operate a church. It takes more to launch a program of evangelization. Much of the financial support for projects of and among the younger churches has been given by the older churches, and in the expenditure of money from older churches by the younger churches tensions have arisen. Parallel situations in family life are so common that any amplification is unnecessary. The inability of so many of the younger churches to achieve financial independence has in the past produced some of the thorniest differences between younger and older churches. Let the business man, impatient — if he has any interest in missions — for the complete financial maturity of the younger churches, ponder a few facts.

Outside the Christian community there is no other institution like the church. There are other organized religions whose temples are repositories for fabulous wealth compounded of offerings given to appease an angry god, but the church is unique. The church has been a part of Western culture and has molded that culture for centuries. When it is transplanted, however, it is a strange, foreign institution. To people in the lands of the younger churches the role of the church and its pastor is frequently misunderstood. The priest, the holy man, and the monk are known — as professional religionists, and their services are paid for when occasions of necessity arise. But the Christian pastor, entrusted with the continuing care of souls in his congregation, and supported by voluntary offerings, seems to be an anomaly. It is difficult for a convert, himself with only the most meager sustenance, and with scant experience in the Christian church, to think of supporting another whose work he can regard only as unnecessary. A further consideration to reckon with is that converts, who once spent a large amount of money to purchase amulets or to pay for religious services, seldom give a comparable amount to their church. The grateful realization that salvation by faith is the gift of God's free grace, the heart of evangelical testimony, seems frequently to immunize a convert against a real sense of financial responsibility for his church, although he has just been released from the onerous burden of paying heavily for the good favor of the gods. Then, too, many who become Christians in the lands of the younger churches are by that act cut off from former sources of income. In some lands it still costs heavily to become a Christian. All of these factors militate against the rapid achievement of financial maturity by a struggling younger church.

The crux of the whole problem is this: the Western-type church that missionaries have transplanted has been readily supported by people accustomed to a high level of economy. But what happens to a church's financial support when it is set down, with all its auxiliary units, in a land whose economic level is low? True, one must record the remarkable examples among economically depressed people of churches that have been self-supporting almost from their founding, as for example, the churches of the aboriginals of Chota Nagpur, India, of the Karens of Burma, of the Koreans, and of the Bataks of Sumatra. But they are the exceptions. The grave difficulties involved in the financing of the younger churches must be kept in mind when one is considering the financial relationships between older and younger churches.

Serious problems of salary also arise in the countries of the younger churches. In a land not his own, the missionary has special needs that must be met if he is to carry out his work effectively; but the disparity in income between missionary and national doing the same work has in the past been a cause of friction. The same disparity exists, of course — and it, too, is tension-producing — among nationals engaged in Christian work. There are grave inequalities, for example, as between doctors or teachers and ministers. Similar serious differences exist in the salaries paid to nationals by local churches and those paid by Western-supported institutions. The entire question, it can be seen at a glance, is fraught with difficulty.

Whitby, recognizing the impossibility of detailed suggestions, laid down only general principles, the application of which must be left to the wisdom and Christian spirit of the churches involved. The six principles that emerged were a reminder that Christian service calls for self-sacrifice and is always to be regarded as a vocation and not primarily as a means of livelihood. The delegates insisted, however, that all salary scales be based as far as possible on need, and that the minimum salary for each class of workers allow the worker to live adequately.

When one is far from the field where these problems constitute part of the fabric of daily living, and when one reads of them in well heated homes where there is no hunger, one finds it difficult to appreciate the poignant urgency with which the churches must seek to correct certain grossly unfair discrepancies that occur in remunerations to Christian workers. The writers of this book have been in correspondence with a Chinese Christian friend, the father of a family of eight, who remains at his teaching post in a theological seminary even though his salary is sufficient to care for his family's needs for only five days of each month. Because of his ability he has been offered by the government and by secular institutions positions that would allow him and his family to live in comparative luxury. Yet because of his deep commitment, he continues with his work in a Christian institution, when to do so means denying his older children the privilege of college and forcing them to help support him and the rest of the family for twenty-five days of every month. The problem here, as it is in thousands of similar cases, is acute and must be faced boldly.

In surveying the task of the world church one must recall, too, that the war wrought an unusual change in the financial status of some churches. In the past the older churches have been blessed with relatively abundant financial resources, while most of the younger churches have had to struggle to maintain even partial financial support of their work. The war, however, has brought desperate poverty to some of the older churches. Grateful for what has been given to them in the past and moved by the distress of their brethren, some of the younger churches have contributed to the restoration and recovery of afflicted older churches. The stories of such gifts are reminiscent of the offerings from the younger churches that Paul took to the parent church at Jerusalem when that church stood in need.

At Whitby, for instance, the Reverend W. M. P. Jayatunga of Ceylon suggested that younger churches send gifts to the church in Germany in token of Christian love and a partnership shared together. In reply, Dr. Hartenstein of Germany thanked Mr. Jayatunga and related how one church in India last year, when its members heard through a Swiss missionary of the suffering of the German church, used its surplus funds of the previous year for the work of the German church and then sent additional sums of money and food through the Swiss. The Reverend Hickman Johnson of London related how the Methodist Board of Missions in England had received $7,000 from several younger church congregations for the assistance of those who had lost their homes through bombing. The collection for the English began with the suggestion of a child in a Sunday school in Colombo, Ceylon.

Again and again Whitby delegates unanimously underscored the pressing necessity for thoroughgoing education in Christian stewardship in every church. The consecration of material wealth by Christians must be insured by adequate stewardship training. Whitby also called on the younger churches to take every means at their command to increase their own financial resources. When one recalls that not more than 15 per cent of the 55,000 younger church congregations in the world are entirely self-supporting, he can readily see the necessity for immediate consideration and aggressive planning by the younger churches to meet this problem. Training and nurture in Christian stewardship are essential from childhood. Today one must always envision his stewardship against the background of the urgency of the total world-evangelistic task.

But the need for an equally vigorous campaign of stewardship training in the older churches is also imperative. There are literally millions of church members in the older churches whose purview simply does not include any portion of world evangelism. The missionary movement has long been a minority enterprise within the church from the standpoint both of candidates for service in the lands of the younger churches, and of those who voluntarily contribute for the support of missions. The church has been granted a moment of unprecedented opportunity precisely because the world stands in such fatalistic fear of its own diseases. The church can seize its opportunity only when every Christian lives the total stewardship to which his acceptance of God's redeeming grace in Christ commits him.

Partners in Personnel

When a new geographic area becomes the center of an evangelistic task in the lands of the younger churches, the aim must always be to bring into existence at the earliest possible moment a self-governing and self-propagating church. The period of missionary tutelage for such a new church, allowing for the adequate development of leadership, should be made as brief as possible. Responsibility for leadership must then pass from the hands of the missionary to the leaders of the local Christian community. Obviously, the future of the younger churches depends on their local leadership. One must recognize regretfully that in many younger churches the leadership available is not adequate to meet the complex and difficult demands confronting a small Christian minority in a predominantly non-Christian land.

There are many tasks to which the younger and older churches in partnership must give themselves. One is paramount. The task to which absolute primacy must be accorded is the enlisting and training in the younger churches of leaders fully equipped to bear the heaviest burdens. On that point Whitby was emphatic. This means a new determined effort in the younger churches to recruit young men and women for Christian service, to provide more adequately for their training — including both ordained and lay members — and to procure for them scholarships in the great educational and theological centers of the world.

Not without reason, the continuing problem of the younger churches is the recruiting of ministers. Christians in the lands of the younger churches, living on an economic level much lower than that of their fellow-Christians elsewhere, are hard put to support a church and a pastor. Furthermore, the role of the pastor is new in the minds of most people. Young persons are more readily attracted to Christian service in teaching or medicine. Then, especially when a church is weak and dependent, the ministry is not likely to command the attention of the ablest young Christians. But it is only through superior leadership that the churches can be lifted to new levels of spiritual and economic power. A weak church attracts only a mediocre ministry. The primary consideration is to solve this problem, to break the vicious circle that it produces, and to recruit an able ministry. Because this problem cannot be eliminated overnight, the younger churches must place much greater stress than heretofore on training laymen for unpaid positions of major leadership in the churches.

The New Missionary

In the tomorrow that is here the missionary who goes to serve in the younger churches has a somewhat new, yet old, role. In the first place, while retaining the closest relationship with his home church, he should become a member of the church that he is to serve; during his period of service in that church he should give it his full allegiance and consider himself subject to its direction and discipline. In the separately prepared reports of the younger and older church groups at Whitby this point was most strikingly agreed upon, in both thought and wording. The missionary becomes fully a member of the younger church to which he is called and becomes, equally with his brethren in that church, eligible for any position to which he may be summoned by the church.

In the second place, the missionary must be ready for pioneering tasks. There was a time when the missionary broke all the new ground in the lands of the younger churches. Then, as some leadership in the younger churches came to the fore, it became apparent that wherever possible the younger church leaders should be responsible for new work undertaken in their home land. Mission boards made much of the necessity of having the missionary accept a subordinate role and of having him serve primarily to develop indigenous leadership. Much stress was laid upon the missionary "specialist." The encouragement and establishment of local leadership are still, obviously, the primary jobs of missionaries in the younger churches. However, if Whitby made one thing clear, it was that in the lands of the younger churches the magnitude of the immediate task confronting the church demands far more than the leadership now available in these churches plus auxiliary missionary assistance. Pioneers — missionaries and nationals — are needed on every frontier, in geographical areas as well as in the development of new kinds of work.

There was a time when the missionary went into a new field on his own. He was the missionary leader. More recently he has been regarded as ancillary to the national leaders of the younger churches. Today, however, "the missionary," whether Indian or British, Chinese or American, is regarded as an agent of the church universal. He is one of the specially trained members of the "shock troops" of the church. He is commissioned by one part of the church for service in another part. He becomes a full member of the church to which he goes and a co-worker on a par with the nationals of that church. His primary allegiance is to the church in which he becomes a member. And when that church has an important work to be done, whether in teaching, in the pastoral ministry, in administration, or in pioneer evangelism, it assays its available manpower and appoints the man best qualified for the task regardless of the land of his birth. Here it becomes the responsibility of the older churches with their greater manpower in leadership to make available to the younger churches those who by their gifts and talents are best suited for service with the younger churches. No longer does an older church send a "missionary" in the former sense to a younger church. Today it is a case of the world church reallocating its available resources and using those resources where they are most urgently needed.

One such area of need is pioneering in the lands of the younger churches. Korea, for instance, has 40,000 unevangelized villages. People there are open to the Gospel as never before. Korea wants 40,000 Christian evangelists for that work. Now the Korean church is one of the outstanding examples of a self-supporting, self-propagating younger church, but it cannot begin to supply all the workers needed. Korea wants Christian pioneers, whatever their nationality. And one hears the same urgent plea from Japan, from China, from India, from Africa, and from Latin America. This is not the problem of a single denominational mission board. This is not a problem for a national church alone. This is a matter of total mission strategy for the world church in the tomorrow that is here. The church needs more thousands of pioneering workers today than it has needed at any time in its past history.

Partners in Policy and Administration

The main lines of missionary policy were given in the command to make disciples of all nations and to teach them all that Christ commanded. Each church is committed to the total evangelistic task. Today that means the conversion of nominal Christians and the recovery of vast areas that have fallen away from Christianity in the lands of the older churches, as well as the proclamation of the Gospel to those who have never heard it and the winning of them to the Christian faith. There is one task. It is only emphasies that differ in various countries. While the older churches still have much to contribute to the life of the younger churches, they need in the fulfillment of their charge the rich spiritual resources that are being developed in the younger churches. Indeed, part of the wonder of the to-morrow that is here lies in the fact that the church in the United States and the church in England need a Kagawa quite as much as the church in India needs a Stanley Jones. This truth grows ever more apparent.

Opportunities far beyond the good beginnings already made must be created for younger church leaders to visit in older churches, to enter into and understand the life of those churches, to bear their own distinctive witness to numerous congregations, and to meet for consultation with mission boards and church leaders. Already some churches have invited ministers of the younger churches to serve their pulpits as temporary pastors or to teach in their theological seminaries for longer or shorter periods. The time has now come when denominational mission boards should follow the example of some of the great interdenominational bodies and invite recognized leaders of the younger churches to serve as consultants and secretaries for a length of time to be worked out with the church concerned. All such development of these exchanges is to be encouraged.

The inviting of younger church leaders for temporary service in lands of the older churches is never, of course, to be pursued to the detriment of the younger churches. The movement of leaders from younger to older churches and from younger to other younger churches must always proceed within the framework of the total world mission of the church. The allocation by priority of available personnel will be to those areas where that personnel will most effectively aid the total mission. This is the new two-way movement of "missionaries" in the tomorrow that is here.

Today church leaders are working in a new frame of reference. The recent past has seen the emergence of a world church — an ecumenical Christian fellowship as broad as the inhabited world. Increasingly, those who serve the churches will do so with a consciousness of their allegiance to this fellowship rather than to a particular denomination in a particular country. The old distinction between the national pastor and the "missionary" is rapidly disappearing. Both are laborers in a particular country for the church of Christ whose Gospel is for all the world. In the same way the old distinction between "sending" and "receiving" churches and "older" and "younger" churches is passing. Yet in accordance with God's provision of varying gifts in different individuals that Paul understood so well, in the tomorrow that is here different members of the world church will have varying responsibilities and contributions.

The course of Christian history makes one evident fact of today outstandingly significant. In the years ahead responsibility for leadership in world-wide Christianity will pass more and more to the churches today designated "younger." Thus it has always been. And the rapid rise of the younger churches in the last forty years to a position of influence in world Christianity makes the movement all the more apparent. The tomorrow that is here is the tomorrow of the younger churches.

Chapter Seven

NEXT STEPS

WHAT ADDITIONAL CONCRETE STEPS SHOULD BE taken to carry out the obligations that are placed on Christians of both older and younger churches by the eternal Gospel in the tomorrow that is here? Whitby recognized the responsibilities. It faced the urgent challenge. It took account of the resources that are to be found in the Gospel and the world-wide extent of the church. It then outlined the next steps in the world mission of the church. At first sight some of these may appear pedestrian and dry. However, for those who are willing to exercise their imagination and to try to see behind the bald statements something of what each involves, they become exciting, even breath-taking. In naming them, logical order is difficult if not impossible. All are important.

Evangelism

First of all, every feature of the program was designed to reinforce evangelism. Evangelism was the major emphasis of Whitby. By evangelism is meant obedience to the Great Commission. This includes not only preaching but also making disciples and teaching the observance of the whole range of the commands of Christ. The commission is as broad as the human race. To carry it out completely would transform all human life. Although the delegates at Whitby were relatively few and fully aware from hard personal experience of the power of the forces opposed to the Gospel, they dreamed and planned in terms of the inhabited earth. Although many of them were administrators, responsible for carrying through what was recommended, they did not quail before the Herculean assignment.

Literature, Visual Aids, Movies, Radio

In the proclamation of the word, both old and tried instruments were recommended and new devices were singled out for attention. The Bible, as always, was foremost. Because of the war, a shortage of Bibles has developed in more than one country. The supply must be replenished. Further aids for teaching the Bible must be developed. Other Christian literature must also be produced. The need is partly for the discovery, encouragement, and training of authors and partly for obtaining a wider circulation of the literature that already exists. Among the new devices are the radio and visual aids, including moving pictures.

Race Relations, Rural Life, the Family

All aspects of life demand the attention of the church if it is to be true to the entire scope of the Great Commission. One of the most clamant of these, obviously, is race relations. Many missionaries are addressing themselves to the problem in one area or another, and in some places progress is being achieved. Among these encouraging instances are sections in the South of the United States and even in South Africa, where the tensions are as acute as in any place on the face of the earth.

What is often termed rural reconstruction is another major challenge. The vast majority of mankind live in rural areas.

They must be reached by the Gospel and the fabric of their lives made over. To do these things, education must be adapted to the need of the people, methods of agriculture improved, family relations bettered, and a community centered about the church.

Not only in rural but also in urban areas must the church address itself to the family and seek to permeate it with the Gospel. So far as possible, the entire family must be Christian. Too often the individual has been won while his family has remained outside. Christian ideals of courtship, marriage, home life, and the rearing of children must be inculcated.

International Relations

Of major importance to our age is the field of international relations. In more than one way the churches have been active in promoting better order among the nations. Of first-class significance has been the fashion in which the world-wide church has maintained and strengthened its fellowship during the wars and tensions of the present century. The presence of the missionary has made for a "reservoir of good will." In hundreds of local congregations mission study classes have brought sympathetic understanding of other peoples. Through its Commission on the Bases of a Just and Durable Peace, the Federal Council of the Churches of Christ in America has been stimulating and coordinating thinking in the United States on the application of Christian principles to the international scene. In the summer of 1946 there was instituted, by the International Missionary Council and the World Council of Churches, the Commission of the Churches on International Affairs. Thanks largely to the initiative and energy of its director, Professor Nolde, it is already making headway, through the United Nations, on the vexed issue of religious liberty. Its activities must be enlarged to bring the informed collective opinion of the churches to bear on the international situation.

Schools and Hospitals

Clearly those characteristic features of missions — schools and hospitals — must be continued. In some countries the government is gradually taking over these responsibilities, but in other countries missions still provide most of the modern medical care and the larger part of the schooling. Even where the government carries the major part of the load, the Christian forces must pioneer in new ways and with fresh methods. Schools are one approach to the intelligentsia. If the church is to be faithful to its commission, it must win to its side the best minds of the country. Providing schools is one way of accomplishing this purpose.

We must add that in every land, whether of the older or the younger churches, one of the pressing and constant problems is to keep Christian schools and hospitals Christian. For many reasons, the drift toward secularization is strong. Those in authority must always be on the alert, not only to check the drift but also to improve the Christian quality of the institutions.

Personnel

Of primary importance in evangelism is personnel. In our survey of the world we met this in country after country. In the lands of the younger churches, as we saw in the last chapter literally tens of thousands of men and women, both clerical and lay, are needed, not only to staff existing congregations but to reach out in untouched areas and groups. Among the unevangelized are thousands of villages, many industrial centers, and great sections of the intelligentsia. To reach these, personnel must be enlisted and trained. Moreover, financial support must be found. Some of this aid will come from the older churches, but the economic base of the younger churches must be so broadened that self-support can be achieved. In many places, as we have suggested, this will entail a form of organization different from that in the older churches, with greater responsibility on trained laity than is usual in the latter.

At Whitby the representatives of the younger churches were insistent in their request for missionaries from the older churches. The number imperatively needed totals thousands. When one recalls the small minorities that most of the younger churches constitute in their respective lands, the reason for the demand becomes clear. Missionaries must be provided to fill needs that the younger churches as yet are too small to meet on the large scale that the urgency of the situation demands. They are required for immense areas where the name of Christ has never been known and where the only hindrance to the preaching of the Gospel is the lack of a messenger. They are needed to take advantage of opportunities in lands where at present marked open-mindedness prevails but may not continue for more than another ten or fifteen years. They are wanted for areas, such as those of the mass movements among the depressed classes and the hill peoples of India, where thousands are being gathered yearly and where more would come if only adequate provision were made for instruction and shepherding. They are requested, too, to help in training leaders. The very best from the older churches are demanded. By "best" is meant not only native ability, although here the standards must be of the highest, but also and primarily Christian devotion and character.

Here mention must be made of the importance of providing fields for German missionaries. Through the late war many areas that had been German mission fields became closed to them. Yet hundreds of German youths are offering for missions and some of the funds for their support have been subscribed. Outlets must be found for qualified German candidates. This may mean financial assistance from other older churches.

The Orphaned Missions Fund

This discussion of German missionaries leads to a discussion of the Orphaned Missions Fund. As we have seen earlier, through a magnificent outpouring of aid that transcended denominational and warring national barriers, that Fund saved numbers of lives and many units of the missionary enterprise. Part of the need has passed. With the ending of the war, contacts have been restored between the missionaries and their home constituencies. Gradually an appreciable number of German missionaries have been repatriated. However, it is still impossible for German societies in particular to secure exchange for the support of a substantial number of missionaries still abroad and at work. Thus for some time to come the Fund must be continued so that persons and projects that otherwise might perish may be preserved.

Money

The Whitby program demands money. It requires more extensive funds today than ever before. This is partly because of the rising price level and consequent mounting costs the world around. To maintain the world-wide work of the church today at the level of earlier times would require many more dollars and pounds than it did then. But the church must not be content with its former achievements. To be so would be recreant to the Gospel and the Great Commission. The program, as we have been saying, must be greatly expanded and at once. Such a program calls for the giving of money on a much larger scale than ever before, and by both older and younger churches.

Priorities

Are there any priorities in this program? Shall the church specialize in areas where the opportunities seem to be unlimited and where the numerical returns appear to be greatest? At present and indeed for the past several decades, the folk of primitive and near-primitive culture have yielded the largest returns. Tremendous numerical gains have been made and are being made in the islands of the Pacific, in Equatorial Africa, among the depressed classes and the hill tribes of India, and among the hill tribes of Burma. In China, where the old culture has been crumbling rapidly and spectacularly, the advance has been substantial and the door is open in unprecedented fashion. Because of the unique situation in Japan, that country has suddenly become one where millions, many of their old foundations gone, are ready as never before to listen to the Gospel. Shall we abandon some areas and groups or be content to mark time where the resistance is such that few converts are made, as is true of much of the Near East? To a lesser degree it is also true of the upper castes of India, of the Burmese, and of the Siamese.

The Jews are a special category. Their sufferings, greater than

those of any other ethnic or cultural group in the past decade
and a half, and the fact that thousands have lost all religious
faith, make them singularly compelling. Yet not many have
become Christians. Here and there are exceptions, some notable,
but no striking mass movements of any size are taking place.
In the United States, where the large majority of the Jews
are now to be found, few attempts are being made to win them.
In some church circles such efforts would be discouraged, for
Jews and Christians are held to have so much in common in their
belief in God and in their veneration of the Old Testament that
to seek to win Jews is regarded as impertinent proselytism. Yet
to surrender to this view would be to give up what is essential
in the Gospel. If the church really believes the Gospel, evangelism — regular parish evangelism — must include the Jews.

As the issue of priorities is faced, missed opportunities of other
centuries come to mind. One was the opportunity we had to
convert the Mongols in the thirteenth and fourteenth centuries.
They had built the widest empire known to man up to that time.
It covered much of Asia and part of Europe. Some of the Mongols were Christians, and the religion of the rest was of the primitive kind that easily yields to a higher faith. A few among the
Christians in Europe saw the opportunity and tried to seize it.
Had they succeeded, much of Asia might today be Christian.
But they were too few and went unheeded by their fellows. The
Mongols became either Buddhists or Moslems, and remain so
to this day. Are we now in danger of missing similar opportunities?

In answering the question of priorities we must at once say
that we can never tell where, from the standpoint of the long
future, the most significant gains are to be made. In the sixth,

seventh, eighth, and ninth centuries the peoples of northwestern Europe appeared singularly unpromising material for evangelism. No central board of strategy would have focused attention on them. Yet they were won, and they became the most active center for the later spread of the faith. In the seventeenth and eighteenth centuries the Thirteen Colonies that later became the United States were an unlikely prospect in any comprehensive world Christian planning. Their population was sparse, they were not wealthy, and church members were a small minority. Yet the United States has become the chief reliance of the church for personnel and funds.

In view of this history, and instances might be multiplied, we cannot now certainly tell where, from the point of view of the far centuries, the greatest opportunities lie. What we must do is attempt to press through those doors into regions that seem to be the most clamant, but not neglect other areas where for the moment the returns are slight. We must seek the evangelization of the entire world in this generation.

The Ecumenical Reformation

One priority is clear. The building of the world Christian community must be stressed. Organizationally, this community, as we have seen, is most inclusively represented by the International Missionary Council and the World Council of Churches. Both are young, and the latter, although active, is still technically in process of formation. The budgets of both are small. Neither is equal to that of a large city church. The churches have not yet given liberally to them. Fortunately, each body has attracted able leadership.

One of the current problems is the relation of these two

bodies to each other. The utmost friendliness exists. Many of those active in one are also prominent in the other. Each needs the other. The World Council of Churches, as is natural, is primarily Occidental and is centering its attention on western Europe, where so much of relief is imperative. If it is to deserve its name, however, it must reach out into the entire world and have evangelism at its heart. This necessity its leaders recognize. Provision is made for membership of younger as well as of older churches, with representation of the younger churches in the initial meeting of the Assembly to be held in the summer of 1948 much larger than their numerical size would warrant. Yet the World Council of Churches cannot specialize on the younger churches as does the International Missionary Council. The latter is imperative for the carrying out of the world mission of the church. On the other hand, the International Missionary Council needs the World Council of Churches, for the latter performs functions that the former cannot properly or as readily undertake. Among these are relief to the churches in Europe and the handling of relations with the Orthodox and Old Catholic churches. It seems probable that each will continue its separate existence for at least some years, but that even closer collaboration will be arranged. The problem is largely one of administration. In both organizations the will is present to solve it in a way that will make for the enlargement of the world Christian fellowship and the fulfillment of the Great Commission.

Of supreme importance in any program for the future are the deepening and broadening of the life of the church. The new reformation of which we have spoken is the most urgent of the next steps. Some one has recently termed it the" ecumenical reformation." By that is meant the world-wide extension of the

Christian faith, the carrying out of the Great Commission, and the increasing collaboration of Christians in that commission. Collaboration in the Christian sense makes essential a growing unity in the world-wide church. This does not mean that all Christians must come into one of the existing communions. Nor does it entail uniformity of worship or even of creed. Obviously it must leave room for great variety, for Christians differ in their backgrounds and in their tastes. The unity must be far deeper than organization. Although organization may help unity, it may also impede it. What is of supreme importance is the unity of love that is the crowning fruit of the Spirit. Because of our imperfect human nature this unity is extraordinarily difficult to achieve. Yet it is not impossible. Whitby was a demonstration that it can be attained. It is love that is born of profound and grateful wonder for the love of God in Christ, and of a humble, glad acceptance with a complete dedication to the Giver. And as that love is seen in the Fellowship, binding together men and women of many nations, races, and cultures, the most compelling witness is given to the power of the spirit of God in the eternal Gospel of Christ.

Chapter Eight

MR. AND MRS. CHRISTIAN ENTER
TOMORROW

WHAT DOES ALL THIS MEAN FOR THE MEMBER OF THE local church? What can the church member do to help share in carrying out the Great Commission? What part, if any, can he or she have in insuring that the church shall take the next steps that were outlined in the last chapter?

At present the overwhelming majority of the members of churches in the United States and the British Commonwealth — in other words, those for whom this book is primarily intended — have very slight, if any, interest in the world mission of the church. Their time is absorbed in their business, their family, their clubs, the local church, and the affairs of the community in which they live. Even the pastors have their minds and hands mainly occupied with the problems of their parishioners, of their congregation, and of the village, city, or neighborhood in which they reside. This situation is to be expected and to a certain degree is to be commended. Yet it has meant that the main burden of the world mission of the church has been carried by only a small minority. The total financial contribution of the older churches of Protestantism to the work of the church in the lands of the younger churches — what is usually called foreign missions — has seldom been more than seventy million dollars a year. Most of it has come in small sums, but were only seventy thousand persons of the hundreds of millions of Christians to give an average of one thousand dollars a year each, the total would be met.

The great rank and file of church members do not take the Great Commission seriously. Nor can we expect that they will easily learn to do so. We can hope for an increase in the number of those who do, but unless we have a sweeping reform and revitalization of the church, for many years to come — perhaps not until after the tomorrow that is here has in turn become yesterday — the majority of professing Christians will not pay more than lip service to the obligation to share the Gospel with all men. That will be too late for millions who will in the meantime die without hearing the Gospel. It may be too late to save civilization. Hitherto evangelism overseas has been a peripheral interest of the church; henceforth it must become a central concern of every congregation.

What can those do who really believe in the world mission of the church? Most of those who read these pages are among that number.

First, all must go about their daily tasks aware of the entire world and of the mission of the Gospel to all mankind. This does not mean that they will neglect duties to their families and to their immediate neighborhoods. As a rule, those who are willing to live in terms of the entire world and to help shoulder its burdens are the most sensitive to needs immediately about them. All too often otherwise "good" people are indifferent to the evils in the world at large, and even near at hand. They may not know of them, or, if they know, they fail to acknowledge any responsibility for doing anything about them. Herein is one of the reasons for the mass tragedies of the day. The "Society of Those Who Care," as it might be called, is small. Yet every Christian, if he or she is true to the faith, is automatically a member of it. The Christian's concern must be as broad as the inhabited world. "All must go and go to all."

In the next place, this minority of those who care must not be content with the indifference of their fellow church members. They must seek to enlist the interest of others in the world mission. Every Christian must be an evangelist and the entire church must be missionary. Impossible though this goal may be, we must not be content with stopping short of its attainment. This can come only through a basic, thoroughgoing reformation. The church must be reconverted. It must be reconverted in every generation, but especially in the generation that is here. The world situation is urgent and will brook no delay. The ecumenical reformation waits for those who have this conviction as a burning passion.

In the next place, we must see to it that every local congregation becomes enthusiastically conscious of membership in the world-wide church. This duty, indeed, is a corollary of the obligation of the entire church to be missionary. Each local congregation must dream and work in terms of the world and must be vividly and actively aware of being a vital unit in the universal church. This by no means entails lack of loyalty to a particular denomination. Every denomination has a contribution to make to the universal church. No one denomination is a full expression of the Gospel. Each must become conscious of being part of that fellowship in Christ that is broader than any one denomination or the sum of all the denominations.

One way in which all can contribute is through the giving of money. Attention has often been called to the fact that American and British Christians are spending many times more on nonessential amusements and luxuries than on the spread of the Gospel. This is especially marked in the United States and Canada. The money spent by church members on such items as movies, tobacco, soft drinks, and alcohol would finance the world mission of the church on a scale many times its present dimensions. The contrast is particularly striking between this indulgence by professing Christians and the present dire need for physical relief among the majority of the population of the globe. Stewardship in "the unrighteous Mammon" is one of the primary obligations of Christians. For many it means that "giving" must not stop with a tithe of one's income, but must go far beyond it. Christian stewardship is recognition of the fact that all that we have, whether of time, money, energy, or ability, is a trust, and that in all expenditure we must seek first of all the will of God. This may even mean, in the United States, giving to relief and foreign missions priority over some of the new church construction that is proceeding on so large a scale. In their giving, some of the smaller denominations with few or no wealthy members are a rebuke and a challenge to the larger ones.

Giving must not stop with money. It must include the dedication of life. Indeed, the latter should precede the former, because to the true Christian the use of money is simply a phase of the total commitment of life. If this commitment is genuine and intelligent, thousands more will be offering from the older churches to serve in what is usually known as foreign missions. Parents must dedicate their children as well as themselves to the world mission. As Christians, with that respect for the sanctity of another's life that comes with the Christian faith, they will not coerce their children into this service. Yet they must so surround them with the atmosphere of the Gospel and of the world mission that they will feel response to it to be natural, even though not easy. When children so respond, parents must welcome the response and not, as is the manner of some, be grieved by it and even oppose it. How many of the children in Mr. and Mrs. Christian's church think of being missionaries with the same naturalness they think of being physicians, lawyers, or engineers?

In the yesterday that is immediately behind us, thousands, among them many of the choicest spirits in the colleges, universities, and theological seminaries, were caught up in the Student Volunteer Movement for Foreign Missions and had as their watchword "the evangelization of the world in this generation." That was the greatest outpouring of life for the worldwide spread of the Gospel that the United States and the British Commonwealth have ever known.

The tomorrow that is here demands an even greater outpouring of life for the world mission. It need not be channeled through the Student Volunteer Movement, although that fellowship is recently having a fresh access of life. It need not — indeed, it probably will not — be through any one organization, but through many. Yet, if the church is to rise to this age that is upon us, it must experience the profound renewal and reform that will spontaneously issue in a similar offering of life.

In connection with the amazing day that is called Pentecost and to which later generations have looked back as the birthday of the Christian church, the words of an ancient prophecy seemed peculiarly appropriate: ". . . your young men shall see visions and your old men shall dream dreams; and on my servants and on my handmaidens I will pour out in those days of my Spirit." We often think of visions as the special prerogative of youth. Visions go naturally with the vigor and exuberance of youth. Old age, "when all the wheels run down," seems naturally to be a time of pessimism and of cynicism. Yet there is a quality in the Spirit of God that inspires even the aged with dreams and gives to the visions of youth a special quality. The "servants" and the "handmaidens," whether old or young, "prophesy" — they speak as inspired and empowered by God.

Something of that spirit of prophecy was seen at Whitby. John R. Mott, from his vantage of more than eighty years of watching the working of God's spirit, and in spite of — indeed, through — his extensive and repeated travels, including those of these recent tragic years that have made vivid to him the travail of the world, was the most daring and confident of that daring and confident company. That was palpably because he had allowed himself to be controlled by the Spirit and so to be used by God across the decades in astounding and quite superhuman fashion. The more youthful of the Whitby gathering also saw visions that were world-embracing. They envisioned "the evangelization of the world in this generation" in even more inclusive terms than did the Student Volunteers of an earlier day. They saw that the Great Commission means not only proclaiming the Gospel to every human being now alive, but also making disciples of them and teaching them to observe all that Christ commanded the intimate circle of his followers to observe.

Fantastic? Yes. But so to "the wise" is the Gospel itself. "Where is the wise man? Where is the scribe? . . . Has not God made foolish the wisdom of the world? For since, in the wisdom of God, the world did not know God through wisdom, it pleased God through the folly of what we preach to save those who believe. . . . We preach Christ crucified, . . . the power of God and the wisdom of God. For the foolishness of God is wiser than men, and the weakness of God is stronger than men."

It was through what looked to the prudent like defeat that God worked for the accomplishment of his purpose in the salvation of men. It was thus on that first Good Friday, that first Easter morn, and that first Pentecost. It will be thus in that tomorrow that is here. God's thoughts are not men's thoughts, neither are his ways their ways. His word shall accomplish that which he pleases and prosper in the thing whereto he sends it.

Who will allow himself to be caught up into that company of those who see as God sees and act as he acts? For them, as for their Master, there will often be the cross of seeming frustration and defeat. He has said that those who would be his disciples must daily take up their crosses and follow him. They will know the fellowship of his sufferings. But they will, with him, be God's instruments in that kingdom in which God's perfect will is done and share with him in the wonder and power of that resurrection that is endless abundant life. That life, because it is God's life as seen in Christ, will not be hoarded by those who possess it, but will be given, as Christ's is given, for the life of the world. The Great Commission is possible because it is from God and because the crucified and risen Christ is with those who seek to obey it.

QUESTIONS FOR DISCUSSION

Chapter One

1. Is mankind really living in "One World"? Explain fully the reasons for your position.

2. Describe the characteristics of the revolution in which mankind is caught. Are these the characteristics of normal change? Do they mark the passing of an age?

3. In a very real sense nationalism and secularism are religions. As Christianity is viewed in the totality of its world setting, which is the more serious competitor, the new religions of nationalism and secularism or the old religions as typified by Islam, Hinduism, and Confucianism?

4. How is one to explain the fact that within thirty-five years two world wars with all their attendant horrors have arisen in the countries that have traditionally been regarded as Christendom? Have movements for international peace and human welfare within these countries actually balanced the demonic destruction of life and character wrought by war? Are such movements to be found in those countries regarded as "non-Christian"?

5. What factors underlie mankind's search for security? Can full security be achieved without limiting individual freedom? What constitutes full security for a Christian?

Chapter Two

1. Should the Christian church in the West seek to arrest the apparent decay of Western civilization? Why? What effect in the past has the dissolution of a civilization had on the church?

2. What is likely to be the long-run effect of the decline of Western Europe on world Christianity? What does this mean for the church in America?

3. Are Christianity and communism actually antithetical? If so, how? Can the church flourish in a communistic state?

4. Have Protestant Christians a right to send missionaries to Latin America when that vast region is regarded by many to be already Christian? Indicate the reasons for your position.

5. The impingement of Western culture upon Africa has caused a widespread breakdown of the old African patterns of living. What has this meant for Africa? Is Africa a fairly typical example of what has happened in other non-Occidental lands where Western culture has penetrated? What is the significance of this for the future of the Christian church?

6. Christianity is a world-wide community. How would you convince a skeptic of this fact?

Chapter Three

1. What is the relationship of the missionary society in the local church to the denominational board or society? From this point trace the relationship of the local society to the International Missionary Council.

2. How is one to explain the lack of tension and the complete unanimity of spirit at Whitby in contrast to similar meetings after World War I? Has this any particular meaning for world Christianity today?

3. What would be the value of a local "Whitby"? How would one go about arranging a city-wide or state-wide meeting that would parallel Whitby in its international, interracial, and interdenominational character?

4. Of what significance for the church is the new experience of oneness in a common task between members of the younger and the older churches? What is the task?

Chapter Four

1. What did Jesus mean when he spoke of the kingdom of God?

2. Describe as fully as possible what is meant by love (*agapē*) as the New Testament uses that word.

3. How must the church interpret the eternal Gospel to mankind today? Can the message of the Gospel actually be made meaning-

ful to all men? What danger lies in seeking to translate the Gospel into the current idiom?

4. How may it be said that the task of world-wide evangelism is impossible? How may it be said to be assured? Is this a contradiction in terms?

Chapter Five

1. What is meant by a first-generation Christian? In the final analysis, can any Christian be other than a "first-generation Christian"?

2. Is it possible to achieve the full meaning of the Christian experience apart from other Christians? If not, why not?

3. Why is it that one who has experienced the new life in Christ cannot contain it within himself? What evidence do these six testimonies provide at this point?

Chapter Six

1. Describe the change in relationship between older and younger churches that Whitby symbolized.

2. Within the common task, what special emphases are for the older churches? For the younger churches?

3. What problems peculiar to the lands of the younger churches make it especially difficult for churches in those lands to be self-supporting. Has this any bearing upon stewardship training in the older churches?

4. What is the role and what are the distinguishing marks of the new missionary? What is meant by the "two-way movement" of missionaries?

Chapter Seven

1. Whitby placed greatest stress upon evangelism. Precisely what is evangelism and what does it include?

2. What are the major channels through which the churches are seeking to influence government to effect better international relations?

3. What are the needs of the world church for new personnel? What can the local church do to see that these needs are met?

4. Of what importance are geographic or group priorities in the world mission? What is meant by the ecumenical reformation?

Chapter Eight

1. Is there any special way in which your own local church could contribute significantly to the total world mission of the church? In material aid? In ideas? In personnel?

2. Theoretically, ten tithing families can support an eleventh whose energies can be directed solely to the fulfillment of the church's world mission. On this basis, what are the potentialities of your church for supporting workers in the world task of the church? Can you personally do something to improve the situation locally?

3. There is nothing mysterious about a "call" to service in the world-wide work of the church. God can touch the hearts of those persons whose minds are factually and vividly aware of the needs of the church and the world. In light of the imperative need for thousands of the ablest young people, what immediate steps can you take to make known to such young people the poignant urgency with which the younger churches are requesting literally tens of thousands of new workers?

4. From whom is the renewal of life to come in your church?

A REFERENCE LIST

Azariah of Dornakal, by Carol Graham. Fascinating story of the great Anglican Indian bishop. London, Student Christian Movement Press, 1946. 6s.

Advance through Storm, Volume VII of *The Expansion of Christianity*, by Kenneth S. Latourette. A.D. 1914 and after, with concluding generalizations. New York, Harper & Brothers, 1945. $4.00.

Bringing Our World Together, by Daniel J. Fleming. A study in world community. New York, Charles Scribner's Sons, 1945. $2.00.

Can Christianity Save Civilization? by W. M. Horton. New York, Harper & Brothers, 1940. $2.00.

Challenge of Redemptive Love, The, by Toyohiko Kagawa. Nashville, Abingdon-Cokesbury Press, 1940. $1.50.

Christian Global Strategy, A, by W. W. Van Kirk. A challenge to the churches. Chicago, Willett, Clark and Co., 1945. $2.00.

Christian Imperative, A, by Roswell P. Barnes. Our contribution to world order. New York, Friendship Press, 1941. (Out of print, but available in some libraries.)

Christian Message in a Non-Christian World, The, by Hendrik Kraemer. New York, International Missionary Council, 1947. $3.50.

Christian Mission in Our Day, The, by Luman J. Shafer. A realistic consideration of the place of the church in the postwar period. New York, Friendship Press, 1944. Paper 75 cents.

Christian Missions in Today's World, by W. O. Carver. New York, Harper & Brothers, 1942. $1.50.

Church Faces the World, The, edited by Samuel McCrea Cavert. New York, Round Table Press, 1939. $1.50.

Church Must Win, The, by Charles T. Leber. The place, power and promise of the Christian church in the conflict of our time. New York, Fleming H. Revell, 1944. $1.75.

Committed Unto Us, by Willis Lamott. The challenge of evangelism today. New York, Friendship Press, 1947. Cloth $1.50; paper $1.00.

Evangelism. New York, Department of Evangelism, Federal Council of the Churches of Christ in America, 1946. 10 cents.

Evangelism, Volume III of the Madras Series. New York, International Missionary Council, 1939. $1.50.

Evangelism for the World Today, by John R. Mott. A symposium of viewpoints. New York, International Missionary Council, 1939. $2.50.

Family and Its Christian Fulfilment, The. A symposium published by the Foreign Missions Conference, 1945. Cloth $1.00; paper 60 cents.

For All of Life, by W. H. and C. V. Wiser. This informed and skillful study describes Christian ventures in many lands that seek to bring the gospel to bear on all of life. New York, Friendship Press, 1943. Paper 50 cents.

God's Candlelights, by Mabel Shaw. An educational venture in Northern Rhodesia. New York, Friendship Press, 1945. Cloth $1.25.

Heritage and Destiny, by John A. Mackay. New York, The Macmillan Co., 1943. $1.50.

Highway of Print, The: A World Wide Study of the Production and Distribution of Christian Literature, by Ruth Ure. The opportunity for literature Evangelism. New York, Friendship Press, 1946. Cloth $2.00.

Is the Kingdom of God Realism? by E. Stanley Jones. Nashville, Abingdon-Cokesbury Press, 1940. $2.00.

Kingdom without Frontiers, The, by Hugh Martin. The witness of the Bible to the missionary purpose of God. New York, Friendship Press, 1946. Cloth $1.25; paper 75 cents.

Larger Evangelism, The, by John R. Mott. Nashville, Abingdon-Cokesbury Press, 1944. $1.00.

Living Religions and a World Faith, by W. E. Hocking. New York, The Macmillan Co., 1940. $2.50.

New Buildings on Old Foundations, by J. Merle Davis. A handbook on stabilizing the younger churches in their environment. New York, International Missionary Council, 1945. $1.75.

On This Foundation, by W. Stanley Rycroft. The Evangelical witness in Latin America. New York, Friendship Press, 1942. Paper 75 cents.

Outline of Missions, An, by John Aberly. Philadelphia, Muhlenberg Press, 1946. $3.00.

Pathfinders of the World Missionary Crusade, by Sherwood Eddy. Life stories of forty missionaries, with side lights on the Student Volunteer Movement. Nashville, Abingdon-Cokesbury Press, 1945. $2.75.

Philosophy of the Christian World Mission, The, by Edmund D. Soper. Nashville, Abingdon-Cokesbury Press, 1943. $2.50.

Prayer, the Mightiest Force in the World, by Frank C. Laubach. New York, Fleming H. Revell, 1946. $1.25.

Religious Liberty: An Inquiry, by Searle Bates. New York, International Missionary Council, 1947. $4.50.

Shrine of a People's Soul, The, by Edwin W. Smith. A story of the little known work of missionaries in many countries who have mastered unknown tongues, reduced them to writing, and given the Bible to their peoples in translation. New York, Friendship Press, 1947. Cloth $1.50; paper $1.00.

Silent Billion Speak, The, by Frank C. Laubach. Literacy in evangelism. New York, Friendship Press, 1943. $1.25; paper 75 cents.

Sir, We Would See Jesus, by Dr. Daniel Thambyrajah Niles. A study in evangelism. London, Student Christian Movement Press, 1938. Paper 2s.

They Found the Church There, by Henry P. Van Dusen. The armed forces discover Christian missions. New York, Charles Scribner's Sons, 1945. $1.75.

Way of the Witnesses, The: A New Testament Study in Missionary Motive, by Edward Shillito. New York, Friendship Press, 1947. Cloth $1.25; paper 75 cents.

Witness of a Revolutionary Church, The. Statements issued by the Committee of the International Missionary Council at Whitby. New York, International Missionary Council, 1947. 20 cents.

World Christianity, Yesterday, Today, and Tomorrow, by Henry P. Van Dusen. A summary of the historical interplay of Christian unity and the enterprise of missions, with a clear-cut view of trends in contemporary Christianity. New York, Friendship Press, 1947. Paper $1.00.